The SPIRIT of the POND

The SPIRIT of the POND

TOM O'REILLY

MACMILLAN

First published 1996 by Macmillan
an imprint of Macmillan Publishers Ltd
25 Eccleston Place, London SW1W 9NF
and Basingstoke

Associated companies throughout the world

ISBN 0 333 64932 X

9 8 7 6 5 4 3 2 1

A CIP catalogue record for this book is available from
the British Library

Typeset by Florencetype Limited, Stoodleigh, Devon

Printed by Mackays of Chatham PLC, Chatham, Kent

In memory of Rodney Morgan, last of the gentlemen
anglers, and to Bernie Skuse, poet and
poacher king.

Acknowledgements

I would like to take this opportunity to express my gratitude to all the people who helped me with every aspect of this book.

To my Mother, Father and brothers Jonjo and Toby for all their encouragement. Marilyn for all her countless hours typing, Lizzy for checking the text and Georgina at Macmillan. To my good friend Guy for his patronage. To my angling companions Paul 'Tails of the river bank' Taylor and Alan 'not worthy of a MK IV yet' Osbaldeston. To my sponsors Agutter's of Ashford in Kent for making me such a beautiful pair of canes; and sincere thanks to the Earl of St Germans for the freedom to roam his estate.

Lastly Claire, my loved one, for her full support and commitment.

Thank you all.

CONTENTS

The SPIRIT *of the* POND

Angling is all about learning;
not just about fish, but
about nature and the
world around us. The whole
feeling and spirit of fishing is about being at one
with your surroundings, merging and disappearing into all
things rural and peaceful. Described on the following
pages is a very special relationship between an angler and
his love. It follows a year in the life of two ponds and all
its inhabitants, plotting the seasons and watching the
changes which occur.

The experiences you will read about are all true,
the views and observations you may or may not agree
with.

The fish are in no way massive or of record size, they

are just part of that special relationship and are the very best the Pond and the Blown-up can offer. However, as all the best and most contented fishermen know, it's not the fish that count.

Without fishing, my life would be incomplete. To catch every big fish imaginable, my life would still be incomplete — such is angling!

The ponds around which I grew up hold a certain magic which, for me, no others hold: memories, nostalgia and changes are all held very dear to my heart, forever dwelling on that missed chance and the one that continues to be elusive.

I |

'Lithiack', an old dairy designed by Humphrey Repton stands only a stone's throw away from the water's edge. This is where I grew up. As a child, I was perpetually exploring unknown parts of the Pond which the average passer-by would never have dreamed existed. Secret passages were made in forests of bamboo that only a select few knew about. Hideouts and dens were scattered around the Pond behind the reeds; tree-houses looked down on lazy carp on summer days. The best tree-house was one in a very large chestnut tree which stood on the corner of the dam side. Crisp autumn days were passed collecting conkers from this mighty tree and the summer days in climbing up to the very top and looking for miles (or it seemed miles at the time) across to the estuary on the other side of the fields. Now the 'conker' tree is gone – blown over during that terrible storm in the winter of 1987.

My earliest memory of the Pond is of my father teaching me how to fish and from that day I have never stopped. In my early days of fishing, when I was about seven years old, I used to be a specimen tiddler catcher and would often beat the match fishermen at their own game! The tackle I used then was very simple and still is to some degree, but now I choose to fish this way and I didn't then. My rods were of heavy solid fibreglass, my reel cheap, yet perfectly adequate, a fixed spool. I can't even remember its name! I can remember how I longed for a Mitchell reel and an ultra-lite hollow glass rod. But pocket-money at that time wouldn't allow for such things. Only the bare essentials were needed. Everything else was only dreamed of, and later on, just as I was beginning to get myself a decent set-up, it was stolen from one of the out-houses. This included my two-layer wooden tackle box which I bought when I visited my grandparents one summer holiday. I remember how heartbroken I was – I was left with absolutely nothing, and it had taken a great deal of my hard earned pocket-money to save up for my tackle box. Soon after the theft I managed to buy a few bits and pieces, and a sound investment from my father was required to buy a new rod and reel.

I was catching small roach from very early on. I can't remember any carp. At the time, everyone like me fished for rudd, roach, perch and gudgeon. I used to find in abundance floats that fishermen had lost, which would always please me as it would save my pocket-money from being spent. But today nine out of every ten anglers are carp fishermen and the only things I find now are bomb weights miscast up trees and in bushes. I can remember one or two anglers who did fish for carp. They were the first to use such things as electronic bite alarms, two or three rods fishing at once and bivvies. Being a child I would ask such questions as what happens if the alarms all go off at once!

I would talk to the fishermen and I would very often strike up a good friendship. I'd visit them every time they fished and they would give me tips and advice and even sometimes their old tackle, which was brilliant for a young boy with limited funds. I still go down and talk to the anglers, but now it's talk of big fish, mostly lost ones, and not the fascination of learning new techniques in a new and exciting sport like when I was a child. I used to sit for hours watching another fisherman's float, and count-ing the number of fish he caught, always hoping that I would do the same. I often think how once you've said the first line to an angler, 'Have you caught any yet?', he will be a friend for life. That opening sentence leads the way to friendship, to fishing trips, to unexplored ponds and rivers and sometimes to unexpected bargains. Today, looking back, I think I used to have far more patience watching someone else's float than watching my own. Somebody else's float seemed to have more magic and, indeed, there is magic in the bobbing of a float.

What else can keep a person active and addicted to a passion? The float is an angler's lifeline between reality and dreams, the link to another world and dimension which leads to lifelong happiness. It's almost as if the float is hypnotic — watching a float for hours at a time leads an angler deeper into his obsession which is fishing.

Today, as they sit behind a formidable battery and artillery of rods and reels, waiting for a fish to take their bait that sit fixed to the bottom by three ounce leads which will then sound an electronic bite alarm, modern carp anglers forget about the hidden powers of a float. The alarm will cause the carp fisherman to fumble and fuss with such timed commotion that it will result in missed chances! Now if this angler was used to striking and reacting to a roach bite when using a delicate float, the timing of the strike would be exact.

Just the other day a well-known local carp angler came and asked how I was, while watching me fish for a rudd. He said in a very sarcastic tone of voice, 'Why are you fishing for tiddlers, you should be fishing for carp on a day like this!' To him all other fish are a 'time-waste' and 'nuisance', but I assured him that not only is fishing for different types of fish less frustrating than fishing for carp (which is frustrating at times), but through fishing for 'tiddlers' my stalking for carp has developed into a fine art because the strike is so important. Through fishing for smaller fish, timing and judgement are greatly improved.

As a child, however, I didn't realize about such things. Hot summer holidays soon passed as I watched the Pond change and my fishing repertoire grow, as many roach and perch passed through my keepnet. And I mean passed through! I can remember once having a good morning's fishing, catching twenty or so fish, when a friend of the family walked past me. Being very pleased with my catch, I decided to show it to her, but to my surprise the keep-net which an old angling friend had given me had a big hole in it and all my fish had escaped. Much to my chagrin; I am sure she thought I had been telling a 'fisher-man's tale' about my splendid catch.

I can't remember my first carp. I've got a feeling it was one of about two and a half pounds and from the Pond, and I caught it when I was about ten. Back then I never used to take photographs, either of myself or of the fish I caught, which is sad in a way because now I have no record of monster fish, only memories. Nowadays I sometimes think that all I go fishing for is the snapshot which will put my face into the fishing press. In fact, I can't remember anyone here taking photos of their fish when I was small, not even the carp men!

When I think back and remember the Pond as it was then, it always seems to be sunny, like when my friends and brothers used to swim in it when there were no anglers about. I once cut my stomach and chest open after diving from the sluice gate and hitting an old bucket which was on the bottom. I dragged myself from the Pond and stood up on the bank and saw that my whole upper torso and thighs were covered in blood!

On one sunny evening in particular, it was the time I had a small rowing boat (I now use a twelve-foot Indian canoe). My father was showing a friend and me how to be safe around boats. He'd given us about an hour's lecture (or it certainly seemed that long) about getting in and out of boats and then gave us the rope to hold as he showed us how to get in. Of course we forgot to hold the rope and my father fell in! He was furious, but instead of shouting at us he just got out and stomped off home, leaving us to find out about boats for ourselves.

Throughout the winter was school. I was average at my work, but excelled in art, mostly drawing fishing scenes (not much has changed). Throughout my secondary education, fishing slowly became my second love – cricket was my first! By the time I was fifteen, I was playing for my County, Cornwall. Unfortunately, due to a heavy tackle playing rugby one day, my cricketing days came to an end. I'd also discovered the opposite sex which made me lose my bearings totally. I often wonder if I could have been a professional cricketer and played for a larger County, maybe Hampshire (close to the Avon) or Worcestershire (fairly close to Redmire). Now I'm called out of early retirement to play in charity matches every now and again.

When the cricket was over, fishing once again reigned supreme. Missing school on hot summer days to go floater fishing for carp, with the 'old crust'; getting parents to drive me and my friends to distant ponds . . . happy days! Summer days turned into nights as my father promised to take me night fishing, which looking back was far more of a camping expedition than fishing. It was both exciting and a little scary because the dark is not something to be laughed at. Night-time is when demons and ghosts and monsters come out of the shadows to scare young anglers, and when evil Cornish pixies tangle lines and make torch batteries go flat for no apparent reason. But I had my guard dog, Bracken, a beautiful red Irish Setter who was the grandmother of Jess, my current companion. Bracken was more likely to lick or ignore an intruder than to attack him! Sadly, Bracken died when I was fourteen years old, thus ending a friendship that I had enjoyed since I was born.

Today the Pond is still very much as it was when I was small. The weed growth in the summertime is far worse than before, though, and one or two trees have fallen down. Anglers have been and gone, as well as friends. A new generation of carp anglers inhabit the Pond. They spend days, even weeks, at the waterside. Indeed, I have every admiration for this type of angler – it shows dedication and patience far more than my way of fishing. But just as people are different, different styles of angling develop and I think you can tell an angler's personality by the methods and tackle he uses. In today's carp anglers, it is often very clear who are the innovators and who are the followers. I myself follow the sacred scriptures carved in pen and ink by Walker and BB; with just a little Fred Taylor and Mr Crabtree thrown in for good measure. I long for the days when fish meant something more than just a number or a photograph. The day when the simplest tackle caught the biggest fish (although sometimes that is still the case).

The Pond has seen many changes and many anglers; they come and they go as one day perhaps I will.

2 |

Sunny one minute, downpour the next, that's what sort of day it is, and windy and cold with it. A typical April-showers day.

I've walked to a small tidal river called the Tiddy. I've always fished here ever since I was little, so-called trout fishing using any method. Today I am using a float with a centre pin, gently trotting a worm through all currents and eddies.

I remember seeing a sea trout run in September 1989. At first I thought someone was swimming as a large splashing came down the river, but as it came closer I could see that it was trout leaping and jumping, all fighting for a front position.

I quickly turned from where I was standing and ran every inch of the way home. I hurriedly grabbed a rod, reel and tackle box, and ran all the way back. The fish were still there. As they cruised past the bank I could see them in full detail, their silvery bodies sparkling like water itself, and their size and number (which I found impossible to believe on such a scale in a river like this).

An old friend who passed away a few years ago, and who lived in the lodge by the river, used to poach here and would often bring me salmon and sea trout weighing over ten pounds. But these trout were massive! I rigged up a rod and tried a worm, but to no avail. I swapped to bread with no joy either. Eventually I turned to a spinner, not even this would produce a fish. Thinking back, the best thing I could have done was to jump in — well maybe not!

Back to today's events. While writing the above passage my float disappeared out of sight and pulling up my rod I find that the float is stuck. I walk down the bank and find it wrapped around a sunken log so I reel in the access line and try to release it. I tug at it and pull harder and harder until the line breaks and the rod flies back with such a force that it hits an overhead branch. A millionth of a second afterwards I think to myself, 'Lucky that didn't snap the tip!' As I turn and focus on the top of my rod I hear a splash. My heart falls and hits the bottom of my stomach. Five inches of split cane and top ring slowly floats and sinks into the river. I walk back along the bank, examine my rod, sigh very hard, and collect my

PERFECT END

things together . . . the end of a not so perfect morning's fishing.

As I trudge back, I think of how many other rods I have snapped, and the more I think about it the more I remember. I seem to spend most of my spare time, apart from fishing, fixing top eyes, taking them off a lesser rod to mend another, and re-whipping. I enjoy this, it's another aspect of fishing. In fact, I would say as much as 80 per cent of my rods have different eyes or are a few inches shorter than they should be.

A friend snapped a roach rod once while trying to land a fine specimen of a branch, so I re-whipped it and now use it as my toughest of tough stalking rods. I can use it up trees, in reeds, in heavy rain, in brambles, in anything that might be a threat to the appearance of the usual rods, and I might add it has landed far more fish!

I am not at the age of remembering split cane rods being sold in tackle shops. I've grown up being surrounded with fibreglass, kevler and duplon, so split cane is a fascination. I love the feel, the smell, and most of all the colour of these rods. Many of my rods are different colours – I've a Mark IV which is as dark as mahogany – but on the other hand I've got a few beautiful Hardy Wallis Wizards, one of which I've just snapped the tip and it's one of my favourites, the colour of corn fields, hot sun and hazy summer days, all with that beautiful red whipping. Although many of my carp rods are becoming

unreliable because of their age, they *set* and *warp*. So I've had a pair made for me called *The Spirit of the Pond* by Agutter's of Kent. These are made with traditional techniques and I can be 100 per cent sure of them.

Being the age that I am I have grown up with the carp revolution. My younger brother, Jonjo, uses optonics, rod pods and bivvies, and camps out for days at a time. He over baits with boilies, weaning the carp from traditional baits. To me this all seems too much, especially the amount of tackle and the cost of it!

I've stalked the Pond for half an hour, lost one fish and caught one in its twenties, yet I've seen other fishermen on the Pond in the same swim every time they come, not even bothering to take time to move around and spot a fish. They arrive here, offload a mountain of tackle, bivvy up and sit and wait for two or more days without a bite. This always seems strange and ludicrous to me. For instance, an angler I often see uses camouflage, even wears it (probably eats it as well!), but then he always parks his bright orange car right next to his bivvy. It's as if he's in a different world and his car was a thousand miles away, not five feet! His is a hypocritical world, one of the hunter and the hunted, a world of survivors and losers, with his car always parked close by to give him a sense of security in case the night is too cold or it rains too hard.

One of the reasons I've been fishing in the river today is because the Pond is too full and I can't get up to my old stalking tricks in my favourite places. So now I'm here at this tiny river, to get away from it all and from the modern carp fishermen who look down on you if you're not using boilies.

If I fish for roach and rudd, I'm looked down upon by the hierarchy of match fishermen who assume that you can't catch a fish without wearing endorsements or baseball caps. I think the anglers today don't have enough variation, enough different types of fishing. A friend of mine says that his method of variation is to fish for carp in big gravel pits instead of smaller ponds. But this isn't very different, he uses the same tactics, same baits, even fishes the same species of fish!

I've seen so many youngsters try fishing for carp, thinking all they have to do is throw a few boilies out in order to catch one. I've seen lots of these children, even men, spend all their pocket-, birthday- and Christmas-money buying so-called carp essentials, and then just give up fishing because they don't catch any carp over forty pounds! However, if they started off like most big names in carp angling, catching roach and bream and so on, it would give them some background knowledge about fish and circum-stances. It's far easier to learn to unhook a three ounce roach than it is a twenty pound carp! With all this in mind I'm sure that anglers with such a varied knowledge wouldn't be discouraged and wouldn't give up carp fishing so easily as a beginner starting carp fishing from scratch.

The day is now starting to brighten up. It's stopped raining and the sun's warming up. In fact I'm very hot underneath my wax jacket. Jess, my faithful companion and man's best friend, is laughing with joy as we walk along the path home. She disappears one minute, pops out the next, runs with all her might and dives back under cover, only to appear many yards in front of me. She gives me a look as if to say, 'Hurry up for I want to get home!', but it's soon forgotten as she turns with speed and follows a scent through the leaves and mud that make up the track. I decide that the look she gave me is to slow down because she is enjoying the walk too much, and there are far more

PERFECT END

things for a dog to do in the middle of a wood than sleeping in front of the fire.

I am now just about starting to get over breaking my rod. My mind keeps retracing my actions and how I shouldn't have pulled so hard, how I should have looked out for the tree or not bothered to get my float and just have left it, even though it is one of my favourites. I should have . . . the list goes on and on. Maybe I shouldn't have come fishing in the first place! But then I would have nothing to write about. Also I might have taught myself a lesson, although I very much doubt that! It's not my first snapped tip and I can guarantee that it won't be my last. Maybe I've just learned about another part of being patient, something every angler needs to know.

3 |

I've fished most of my life, even before I heard about such things as rods and reels. I suppose it all happened when I was about six or seven . . . I discovered eels!

I soon became a specimen eel hunter at a very small stream which ran below my house. I would walk upstream, lifting up stones as I went, looking for eels. When I found one I would catch it with my hands, and then after a great deal of excitement put it in a bucket and run and show it to my mother and father, who would be very pleased and say such things as 'Slippery as an eel!' which after a while would tire me and the joke wore off.

The eels I caught were usually only elvers of about four inches long but occasionally I would find a big eel in the deeper water. Finding an eel of about a foot long would always be a bit of a shock, but after being frozen for a while I would immediately start trying to catch it. I would put my hand underneath the fish and flick it on to the bank. That was the easy part. Trying to grab the eel when it was on the bank was harder. It would slip and wriggle out of my grasp as only an eel can, and slide through the undergrowth like a snake leaving me pulling up leaves and grass in its wake!

Once I had put an eel in my bucket and it had been through the ceremony of being exhibited to my parents I would always put it straight back into the water, although my father said on many occasions – and sometimes still does – that he would eat a big one and how nice they taste.

I've never seen the point of killing fish to eat, even trout or salmon. In the world we live in today a supermarket can supply anything including game fish. I can see the point of getting pleasure from eating something 'wild and fresh', something actually caught by the consumer, but somehow in today's society I find it a little false and pretentious. I much prefer to see the fish go free, whatever type, and it gives me a far better feeling than to see it killed. When I watch a fish slowly swimming away, recovering from the ordeal of being hooked, played and taken from its natural surroundings, it gives me pleasure to know that the fish will live to see another day. I suppose in many ways I am anti-angling when people take it to the extent of killing fish for personal pleasure – gaffing fish, which still goes on even with freshwater fish such as pike.

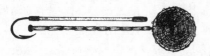 I can remember the days when fishermen always used to kill eels if they caught them while fishing for rudd or roach because eels swallow bait right down to their stomachs and can tangle fishing line. In fact I saw this happen just the other day – a fisherman actually sliced open an eel's bottom and stomach when it was still alive just to get his precious hook back! The number of times I've revived eels that have been left in the sun to die is countless. Eels can't help their species, just like we can't choose the colour of our eyes and hair. I am positive that there would be an uproar in the angling society if the godly carp or barbel were treated in this way.

If fishing is to live on happily and not to be turned into another 'blood sport' by the media, then some laws and rules should be introduced by the Environment Agency and National Federation of Anglers and other organizations to stop some of the cruel things that go on in the world of angling. I am beginning to see its similarities to that of a stocked trout pond, all bred to be killed, to a pheasant farm, all reared to be shot. I suppose they are all frequented by the same sort of people, old brigadier types, the aristocracy, earls and lords, and the 'ordinary' people pretending they're 'the above' and 'upper class', people who would not know what 'class' and 'culture' is if it came up and kissed them!

Because I live where I do I have a very large pheasant farm nearby where the birds are bred to be shot. It makes me very sad and upset to see these magnificent and beautiful animals being preyed upon by mankind. Someone once told me that it's the way of the country and I shouldn't live here if I don't like it. But it's the way it's done that I don't like. The pheasants are let out in such numbers that a blind man could end the day with a bag full of birds. No skill is needed or involved in hunting the birds.

THE FUTURE OF FISHING

A gun can fire hundreds of shot all at once, so you don't even need a certain degree of accuracy!

One year the game farm tried to put a lot of ducks on the Pond ready to shoot when the season started. When the season did start all the ducks hid behind the reeds and the beaters and dogs couldn't get them out to shoot, so now all the ducks eat my bread when I'm fishing. Luckily I haven't caught one yet, but many other fishermen have, and they've put *them* straight back after being unhooked!

Only a minority of anglers are cruel to fish, and these are dying out, but not before time. Many of today's fishing tackle companies and the big names in angling are at last realizing that fish need to be looked after in order to grow and stay healthy. After all, all anglers – even I – want to catch bigger fish and they won't grow if they're unhealthy.

As I've said before, I'm all for improvements in today's tackle, even my old wooden landing net has a knotless mesh to prevent scale damage. So even us 'old-style' fishermen can compromise with modern techniques!

Besides gaffing fish there are many other things that can cause damage. A lot of fish are damaged and hurt by inexperienced anglers using line which is too heavy or too light. Here in Cornwall, surrounded by coastline, it is quite common to find anglers fishing on a lake using sea tackle, but thirty-pound line and thirteen-foot beach casters can cause considerable damage to coarse fish, especially around the lips.

It's quite strange really. Although I'm surrounded by the sea and only live three or four miles away from the coast, I've never been sea fishing in the whole of my life. I've got Plymouth on one side and Looe on the other, which both offer all the opportunities there are, especially conger and shark fishing. I've never even tried coastal fishing for mullet or wrasse. A few days ago I drove to Rame Head, a local coastal landmark, to watch the sun set and I ended up watching a sea fisherman spin for mackerel. I thought to myself how nice it would be to fish there,

watching the beautiful sea and the sun, big and orange, slowly setting, with no other anglers to come up and ask you what optonics or flavoured boilies you are using! Just a rod, spinner, landing net and a flask of tea, or maybe something stronger. Perfect!

I expect I might try coastal fishing one of these days. It boasts everything I like most about angling: the solitude, the simple tackle, beautiful surroundings and, of course, plenty of fish – including big eels!

4 |

As springtime slowly ends, the days get longer, the sun hotter and buds start to appear. It seems like for ever waiting for the trees to bear leaves and for the mud to turn to dust. I long for the days when I will be able to walk without my heavy jacket and boots.

I am walking on a path along the river and estuary. The day is cloudy, creating a patchwork of light and shade, with outbreaks of rain. While I walk, I dream of possible future fortune, but as I look around at the sun, sky, hills, trees, water and wildlife, I ask myself why I need money when all this is free. I can hear the main road on the other side of the estuary. It angers me to see the countryside being swallowed up to make room for another development. At this point, when I have the road in view, I turn and walk back down the track, retracing my boot marks to convince myself I've never walked here. The birds are singing, heralding a fine day, the birth of summer. The only thing louder than a cawing crow is the continuous noise of the cars roaring across the Cornish countryside,

helping their drivers' lives go that little bit faster than if using another, more sedate mode of transport.

My camera swings to my side ready to record one-sixteenth of a second of my life. A camera can capture a precious moment, a split second, which no artist can ever recreate. A painter can, I grant you, take many months to complete a painting in his own style and signature which makes his work unique, but to me opening a shutter seems a far easier way to go about things, even though it may take many months, even years — and a lot of patience — to find that perfect moment. Today, however, I have seen nothing to capture my interest except a pair of nesting barn owls in a derelict barn, but they aren't there any more. So many things I've seen have been far too precious or have happened too fast to photograph. Often you don't want to spoil that perfect moment by fiddling with lenses and light meters. I've seen two kingfishers fighting over a mate, carp spawning and mating, huge shoals of sea trout making the autumn run . . . the list goes on and on, only captured by my memory. If I tell anyone, I can see the disbelief in their eyes. As if I would lie about such a thing for the sake of self-glory or to win over a friend!

5 |

Nearly all my fishing is stalking, be it carp or any other coarse fish, and my personal guidelines and rules stay the same. My most important rule is to go where the fish are. This isn't as obvious as it sounds. I have seen many anglers fish in places where I know they won't catch the fish they are looking for. About 60 per cent of my time stalking is spent actually looking for fish. I seem to spend most of my life climbing trees to locate them. Ash trees are the best for this purpose, although they can be a little on the thin side and will bend and sway as if they've been hit by a tornado when you try to reach the top. Beside many ponds there are trees which lean over the water, and this type of tree is my favourite. When I reach the top of the tree I can look straight down into the murky underwater world which so intrigues me.

I find it fascinating to watch fish in their natural environment. I have been known to sit for hours, time just melting away, watching as the fish go on with their everyday existence.

I find carp the most interesting fish to watch. Their huge muscular bodies, effortlessly gliding through snags and weed amaze me. As I sit and watch them, every so often I will throw in a single bait, a worm, some bread, anything I think the carp will eat. They usually take bread as it sinks, especially if it's a flake; worms and other bait which sink faster will not be taken until they have reached the bottom. They upend with their tails at about a sixty-degree angle to the silt then suck the bait up, and if it's not to their taste, spit it straight back out again. Through watching fish in the water, I've noticed that all of them do this. Roach can quite easily spit out a maggot, so it's not just carp. An example of this and a good case-study is goldfish. You will see them sucking up and spitting out gravel.

Studying carp, or fishing for them, can be like waiting for a bus. There may be none for ages, then several will come along at once. I've noticed this happens a lot. Carp tend to move about in shoals of roughly three to six fish, while other fish come to join them for a while and then leave. In some ponds I've seen the same fish, in the same shoal, time after time.

If you study ponds as much as I do, it is soon quite easy to recognize a fish, estimate its weight, be able to tell where it is likely to go and whether it is usually in a shoal or alone. Most of all I can determine the individual personality of a lot of carp and can recognize them by their actions, whether they are timid or aggressive, young or old. I can even tell the places they like to be in! Sometimes when I see a fish I can stalk, I find it easy to tell if it's going to take my bait simply by its gestures and actions, even before I cast my line into the water.

In some waters I see the same fish over and over again. I can tell by its type, either common or mirror etc., and by its size and distinguishing features such as loose scales, ripped fins and the scale formation. Often I've seen fish which I've caught before — it's like seeing an old friend I haven't seen for a while. Sometimes I've seen fish that I'm about to catch!

By being able to recognize individual fish this way I am also able to judge the size of other fish against them. I've just seen a mirror I once caught which weighed twenty-three pounds and the shoal that it's with are all bigger than him, so I can roughly estimate the size of the others, although admittedly judging the size of fish in the water can be deceptive as some fish look bigger than they really are, while others look smaller.

While watching carp they've sometimes got so close to me that all I've had to do is reach out and I can touch them. Many a time I've been tempted to throw a landing net over them, but you'll be glad to know it has never come to that.

Carp are so very unpredictable. I've been standing in a swim before now, the sun behind me casting a shadow on the water, and while I've been tying up my Indian canoe – which usually makes a great deal of noise – carp have cruised by in shoals oblivious of me. But at other times, the slightest noise or movement can cause a fish to swim with great speed in the opposite direction – usually when you're trying to catch it!

I often wonder if carp know what day of the week it is. Monday to Friday I see carp cruise about very happily, swimming, surfacing, jumping around in the Pond especially if the weather is fine. Yet at weekends, when the Pond is fished to the maximum – as many as twelve fishermen on the two and a half acre lake – the carp all seem to disappear, almost as if they are saying 'It's Saturday lads, let's go and hide!'

Sometimes I feel as if the fish know me. When I stalk in my favourite places with the same bait – which I know works – I watch the fish drift past by my bread flake, worm or whatever, nudge it with their snouts and then turn slowly as if to say 'It's Tom again, same old bait, shall I please him by letting him catch me? No!'

I wrote earlier about seeing fish that I've caught before. When I see them swimming about and looking at my bait I feel I can hear them subconsciously talk to me and look at me with an almost arrogant look and I seem to hear them say 'Not today, you've caught me once, and I'm not falling for that again!'

On occasions when I've caught the same fish I always think that my scales aren't working properly if the fish has put on or lost a few pounds. My scales aren't the most accurate in the world anyway. But this doesn't matter, the size of a fish is really unimportant, or so I try to kid myself. I hardly ever weigh my fish to the nearest ounce, I always round the figure off to the nearest pound, or measure it according to what it looks and fought like.

These two measurements usually contradict each other. I've had twenties going on thirties which have fought like doubles and doubles that have fought like . . . Well you know what's next!

For some people carp and specimen hunting is all about personal best. Looking back at the end of a season and seeing the amount of fish caught, the biggest and smallest, the number of times gone fishing and so on can be a very rewarding and a sombre time. Looking back at photographs which evoke memories of hot summer days and cold winter nights fishing and watching the environment of the water change, recording different colours of the water, either gin clear or dark as pea green soup. Watching the trees, bushes and other foliage grow and become lush, only to turn brown, shrivel and fall. Most important of all, though, is looking back and noticing how your own style of fishing has changed, using experiments with new baits and tackle to help in a different area. All of this, memories and research, helps me to come to conclusions about different baits and which are the most effective at different times of the year.

Modern carp anglers often use this method to find out what ingredients, mixes and flavours of boilies work best throughout the seasons.

It is also very interesting and thought-provoking to recall the places you've fished in and what swim site you caught from. This is valuable for next season because it can save time, money and effort catching the fish. With there being no close season, my time for looking back is at the start of the new year when I am getting ready to improve myself for the coming year's fishing.

Many of my favourite baits seem to work all year round. The only thing that changes is whether they are more effective on the surface or on the bottom. Bread, my favourite bait, can be used in many different forms. The crust is ideal for floating (many modern carp anglers forget this and they use Chum Mixer); bread paste and bread flake are ideal for slow sinking, but can often bring smaller species like rudd and roach. All three of these techniques can be used in different situations. Take bread flake for instance. As well as floating on the surface it can be used under water and popped up from the bottom anything from half an inch to sub surface depending on how much line is being used from the hook to the weights, and at what height the fish are. Worms can also be used in a similar way. If they are pumped with air from a hypodermic syringe they float on the surface, but with the addition of weights they can be popped up and used on the bottom. This sort of presentation can bring about the downfall of carp and eels on the toughest of hard waters where other baits don't and won't work.

Although I am a traditional fisherman and try to live my life according to old values – I consider everything old to be better made, with less 'throwaway value' and less commercial value than anything made today – I can still see the point of progress and what it has to offer. For instance, hair rigs, helicopter rigs, CV safety rigs, PVA strings. With all the magazines and videos on the market at the moment it is hard not to notice the fishing innovations. Growing up with this, I can't help trying things out and improvising with them to adapt my way of fishing, like using popped up worms!

Many of today's innovations are very well thought of, like the safety rigs which have saved fish from having split lips due to damage from fixed leads. Even simple things, which at one time were unheard of, are now a godsend, like unhooking mats that save the fish's protective armour of scales by cushioning the damage which can be caused by the fish flapping about on the bank.

I am sure that many of the fish that I've caught over the years would have passed me by, were it not for the fact that carp are now so used to boilies that their defences are down and they become off-guard and unwary of bread, worms and to some extent even sweetcorn. I am sure that this is why I can usually out-fish most of the usual boilie anglers.

Stalking can offer a new dimension to fishing. With stalking you are on the move all the time, creeping and crawling through the undergrowth by a pond or river. This is particularly good if you've got no patience. Although the bad points must be considered, like crouching very still for over an hour and getting infuriated by fish half taking the bait and constantly catching the landing net. (One way I found to prevent this is to use a large flick-up salmon net with an extendable handle which I clip onto my jacket, although now even this net is full of rips some six inches in diameter!) Also it is not unusual for me to tear my clothes and scratch my legs, arms and face. I am constantly full of scratches and cuts, and frequently fall out of trees while stalking fish.

Other fishermen can also be a problem when stalking. If there are too many other people about there can be quite a bit of trouble, particularly if you've climbed a twenty-foot-high tree right next to another fisherman and then fall out straight into the water! It can also be the other

way around. Many a time I've been alone at a pond and have hidden myself behind a bush so that I won't disturb the carp, when all of a sudden somebody has come up and started setting up their tackle right next to me, not realizing I am there. Being as anti-social as I am, I usually leave them to it and creep off without them knowing I've been there at all.

This reminds me of the time I was fishing a pond that I wasn't supposed to. I had the pond all to myself and had found the perfect stalking place. I'd watched the carp swim and feed there all day and had only actually been stalking in this spot for about ten minutes – my bread flake had already been sniffed at a few times – when a carp, the size of which I didn't think possible in this pond, came up, looked at my bait, opened its mouth and was just about to run off with it when a car door slammed and I heard two voices.

I had a millionth of a second to decide what to do – catch a fish and be caught myself, or run for it. I soon decided to do the latter. As I quickly reeled in my bread the carp sat still in a state of shock, not knowing where its dinner had gone. I rushed away from where I was, causing the carp to see me. I grabbed my rod and landing net and ran in the opposite direction to where the voices were coming from. When I got to the other end of the pond, where I was safe, I looked back and saw two elderly women feeding the ducks. I sighed and sat down, my head was hot and sweating and my heart was pounding, making my head ache. The feeling of relief was overpowering!

As I think about it, I can remember another time this happened to me. I was fishing from a tree when I saw someone coming. I instantly threw an expensive and very good Mark IV out of the tree into the bushes below, causing my favourite old Mitchell 300 to snap at its foot. The people walking by turned out to be no more sinister than a couple out on a stroll in the countryside with their dogs!

As you have read, stalking is not an easy thing to do. In fact, I find it far easier to sit behind two rods and wait for a few hours. But you can't beat the thrill and adrenalin rush of hooking a fish while stalking, especially at close range using a centre pin. It's a wonderful experience to watch carp actually taking the bait and studying their reactions to it. I can almost draw comparisons with fly fishing and the way a trout reacts to a fly. Stalking is not the be all and end all of carp fishing, but it is my way.

Stalking fish is not just for use in the realm of carp fishing. I love to walk up and down river banks looking for big barbel and chub, even salmon and trout and it's not just on rivers either. Even on a pond, I can stalk for large rudd, roach and even tench, in fact many species of fish fall for this method of fishing. Observation is the key to stalking. Looking, watching, even listening to find fish and, like all types of fishing a lot of patience and a little luck is needed.

6|

The end of April and the beginning of May is such a beautiful time of year. The trees are showing their new coats of green which are as fresh and crisp as a frosted morning and the hedgerows and banks are covered in spring flowers. Bluebells, wild garlic, campions, buttercups and daisies give the Pond a sweet fragrance only to be overpowered by a scent of banked carp, which can smell of days gone by, of winter and summer carp long gone. It is such a sweet memory, but it can also be a sour, sickly smell, a whiff of which can make your stomach turn upside down.

The sun shining down throws a veil of haze and the heat shimmer has made the carp restless and docile at the same time. The few hot days have brought the temperature of the shallow pond up to the right level and the carp in one of the ponds are jumping and splashing, ready to mate and spawn. At the other end, carp bask in the warmth of the early morning sun, motionless as if stunned or frozen in time, only their gills slowly moving and fins slightly quivering giving me any indication that they are alive.

When I see the carp in this state, and knowing that there are no other fishermen to disturb me, I go home and get my rod, reel, various pieces of tackle and my bait, which will be bread on a day like this. I rush back to where the carp have been basking, force my hook into a corner taken from a crusty loaf and flick it out not half a yard away from the carp. The bread sits on the surface and I crouch behind the reeds and bushes so as not to disturb the fish.

As I sit and watch my bait, waiting for those huge lips to engulf it and the ripples which indicate the downfall of a carp, I think of all the other times that I have done this. I think of earlier this year when I caught a scamp of a fish in the middle of the reeds after a few hot days in February, which is the earliest time of the year I have ever caught anything from the surface. I had been throwing in bits of crust for a few days before, training the fish to take the bait, and then I heard the sound of sucking as the carp took the crust. Like today, I ran home, got my rod and tackle and flicked the bait out. Being winter, the reeds had died back, so when I hooked the little scamp, the reeds broke its path as I brought him into the waiting landing net. I think my first carp was caught this way and I think that the bait was crust as well, but I lost count a long time ago of how many carp I've caught from fishing on the surface.

While I've been reminiscing, a few carp have taken an interest in my bait. As usual they look at it with interest, only to turn away at the last moment. The Pond is very still and the swallows and swifts are skimming and diving into the water that is a deep dark green, almost transparent in places where the sun shines on it.

Then with a splash, a mouth as large as a cricket ball swallows the crust and ripples spread across the lake. I strike up with the rod. As the fish is hooked, which forces the reel to screech, the clutch lets the line out and I pull up on the rod. This gives the fish some side strain to the right to try and stop it heading for the snag, but then it turns and heads in the opposite direction. I reel in slowly, gathering in line at a constant rate. As the carp gets closer to the bank I crouch down and reach for the landing net. As I feel for it my reel falls from the rod – it has slipped the reel seat on the handle – causing panic and frustration. I immediately grab the reel and slide it quickly back into place, the sweat pouring off my face, my heart pumping so fast I can almost hear it. With one hand holding the rod and playing the fish, I try with my other hand to reach out and pick up my landing net. I sink it into the water and slowly lead the fish into it. The carp's huge body, tired and exhausted, tries once more to escape but this time it only gets as far as the net. I drop the rod and lift the fish out of the water, lying it on the bank to unhook it. Using all my strength I carry the fish in the net, along with my rod, to the soft grass behind the swim. I've struggled every inch of the way: the pain and tiredness, both physical and mental, is excruciating. Don't let anyone tell you that fishing is boring and inactive.

I've just weighed the fish and taken a good look at it. It weighs about twenty-one pounds, a beautiful mirror carp which by its swollen shape suggests it is spawn-bound. I've carefully taken a photograph of it next to my wicker creel and the rod which I caught it on. I pour a bucket of water over the fish and take it back to the Pond, place it in a very large keepsack and tie it next to my boat. A friend of mine, Simon Scott, who has a

ANOTHER MORNING STALKING

MSc in fish biology, and has written a few articles for *Carp World*, warns about 'sacking' carp on hot days and for long periods of time. I don't usually sack carp — I feel that it is unnecessarily cruel because it reduces the amount of oxygen in the water. Well, that's my theory — if you want a more scientific and accurate one, you should write to Simon. (I was considering applying for the course which Simon did but went to Art College instead.) As I put the carp into the water I can see more fish basking a little farther out. The reason I'm sacking my fish today is because I've got a feeling that I'm going to catch another.

While I run back to the house and set up again, the carp are still hovering and peering out from the reeds and weeds which cover this corner of the Pond.

Where my canoe is moored there is a tree which hangs over the water. It has actually half fallen down and is standing at an acute angle of about thirty degrees. Since the carp are all underneath the tree, I think I will try a different sort of approach. I lean my rod up against the tree and shin my way halfway up the tree. The carp are still there and are about ten feet away from me. (I'm five feet up and they're five feet out.) Slowly, trying not to make any sudden moves, I pinch some bread onto my hook and carefully dangle it down to a distance of about four inches away from the snout of a carp. It slowly looks at it, gets closer, and then ... I pull up hard trying to set the hook in its mouth. My baited hook is spat out, causing me to lose my balance for a split second and the fish to realize what I'm trying to do. With a flick of its tail and a splash it swims off with great speed.

Luckily, neither I nor the fish have disturbed the other carp. I often find this happening. I disturb one fish and yet none of the others move. (There is also the other side of the coin when all the fish disappear in the blink of an eye.) I re-bait and swing the bread flake to the remaining carp which look almost white in the water. The flake sinks and a carp instantly takes it. As I strike up this time, I feel what seems like a powerful wall. The fish heads for open water which again causes me to lose my balance and I fall straight out of the tree . . . luckily into my boat. The sun might be hot today, but I can assure you that the water isn't! I quickly sort myself out then stand up in the boat, swing and pull the fish towards me. The poor thing doesn't know what has hit him. One minute he's doing a nice bit of sunbathing and the next he's getting a mid-morning snack with a hook in it and watching an angler fall from the sky into a canoe!

The carp is now beginning to tire, so I feel and pull him in closer while fetching my landing net from the holding place in my fishing waistcoat. I flick it up and reaching and stretching I lift the carp under the net. At the same time I heave a sigh of relief and frustration – my back is hurting from falling out of the tree. I unhook the fish and walk to the other end of the boat, step out

and untie the keepsack holding my other carp. Of course by now the mirror carp has revived and as I pull her up she flaps around, struggles and is generally difficult. I place them on the grass and weigh the second carp, which is about seventeen and a half to eighteen pounds. It's a beautiful carp, leather with just a few scales around the dorsal fin. A few quick photos and then I'll put them back. With the camera work over, I put them in the Pond at the pitch nearest my boat, and watch them slowly recover and glide back into the depths.

It's been a strange morning's fishing: exciting, frightening, pleasant and painful! Fishing is often like this. If it wasn't and I was catching fish without such conditions I would definitely give up. I believe that if you put a lot of time, effort and even pain into something, then the rewards are far more enjoyable than if you get the same result without effort.

7|

Poaching is one aspect of fishing I enjoy that little bit more than anything else because it's nerve-racking, frightening and above all, good fun!

For me, poaching is not about taking fish to kill and eat. It is about 'beating the system' and laughing in the face of syndicates, clubs and landowners who make the rules about what an angler can or cannot do. The poacher has no rules, no licences, no membership fees, no barbless hooks, no cereal groundbait, no day tickets and no time limits. The poacher is an angler who takes the rules and law into his own hands and juggles with catching a fish without being caught.

Thoughts of tackle confiscation, fines and bans go through the poacher's mind as he goes about his business, usually with excuses in mind such as 'I didn't know you couldn't fish here', 'I didn't see a sign saying you couldn't fish here', 'So and So said it was OK to fish here', 'My friend lives just up the road', 'I was going to put them back . . . Honest!'

This is the way of a poacher – catching a fish with a little bit more than just skill and patience. The poacher has to have all his senses finely tuned to everything around him; his eyes and ears alert to every breath of wind and any noise out of place, a snap of a twig or a dog followed by its owner. A poacher must react to everything his ears can hear.

Deep down there is an inner consciousness whispering unsaid thoughts into his head. Was that a noise? Then the eyes and ears home in seconds after. The best likeness I can draw is stalking a carp at night-time, the elements are nearly the same, yet the poacher experiences these day and night.

There's so much more thought and consideration that goes into poaching, far more so than ordinary fishing. For instance, how will the poacher get to his chosen site and back? A car would draw far too much attention unless it can be hidden out of sight or left some distance from the pond or river. A bicycle is better, a silent attack, every second planned like a military exercise. But the bike is rather slow if a quick getaway is required, although it can be hidden much more easily. What about walking? Nothing to hold you back, it's silent, you can hear anything or anyone who might be coming too close. But what about distance? Walking is all well and good but what if you want to poach a pond ten miles away? It would take you all day to get there!

There isn't an easy or fail-safe way of reaching the water or leaving it, but on the whole I prefer a bicycle. A good distance can be covered, it keeps me fit, it is silent and can be easily hidden out of sight behind a hedge or gate.

There is a certain adrenalin rush with poaching which draws me back to it: the chance of being caught or not, taking on the odds which are all stacked against the poacher. The only time for relief is when the trip comes to an end after a snapshot has been taken, for a trophy, for a keepsake; a memory which I can share with others as proof of my travels. As I said earlier, I don't believe in killing for fun or for the table and in any case many places I poach aren't for trout and salmon but for carp!

There is a pond a few miles up the road owned by some club or other, which I used to fish on a regular basis, where the carp grow up to weights in the twenty pound mark. The pond is quite deep because it's also the water supply for the local village. The bottom and sides of the pond are made of slate and stone, and there aren't weed or lilies so there isn't much for the carp to eat and they are there-fore always willing to bite. To reach the pond you had to walk through the village and straight past the bailiff's house. (The bailiff controls the pond.) There was no way

I could use a normal rod as it would have been seen, so I used to just wear a big waxed jacket and carry a home-made poaching rod which is three-piece and eight feet in length. It can be carried with a reel inside my 'poacher's' pocket of my jacket, along with a small tackle tin with various sized hooks, weights and so on, forceps for dis-gorging the fish, a weigh sling and scales, a camera and of course the bait which is usually bread because of its versatility.

Once at a pond, poaching can begin. I walk around it first, taking note of possible swims for probable fish. If there are any in casting distance I will maybe try to catch them, if not, I will leave a few small balls of paste so that once I've walked round the perimeter of the pond, the carp will hopefully have found my bait and started to feed on it.

Once I've found a fish I free-line bread flake to the fish, which leaves a trail of bread crumbs in the

water which attract the fish. When I catch and land the fish I weigh and take a photo or two; and then the carp is set free so I can find another.

I sometimes use a hand-line for poaching. This is good not only because all you need for it can be kept in your pockets, but also because it is cheap. If I was about to be caught by a bailiff I could just throw it away in the nearest hedge or even in the water! I would much prefer to buy another hand-line than to use one of my rods and reels and have to treat it in the same way.

I was using a hand-line on one of my best poaching trips, one I hadn't planned as such. It was my loved one's birthday and I suggested that we should go for a walk up to the reservoir which is renowned for its brown and rainbow trout. Claire's birthday is in October, so we decided to take a gas stove and cook some food to help keep the cold out. We walked for a while and when we felt hungry we stopped by the reservoir and I started to cook some sausages. While I unpacked my haversack I found an old hand-line and, thinking nothing of it, I pinched on some bread flake and cast a little way out. I then carried on cooking and by the time I had drunk a cup of tea, I had caught a beautiful autumn, out of season rainbow trout. When we had finished our picnic I had caught four trout, weighing about two pounds each. I put each one carefully back, much to my father's dismay.

I've poached this reservoir a few times now and can strongly recommend it . Because the lake is so big I have never seen any bailiffs or gamekeepers about, and you can avoid the fly fishermen who tend to stay up one end. I find myself a quiet corner and bay which is only visited by cormorants.

To some people poaching is a way of life. In today's society there are still many people who get a great deal of satisfaction from something they have killed or caught. Not only fish, but pheasants, ducks, rabbits, pigeons and so on.

A very old friend of our family, Bernie Skuse, survived almost entirely on things he poached. One evening my father ate squirrel sandwiches with him, which to me seemed barbaric, and I often wonder how little meat there must be on a squirrel. Bernie used to justify his poaching by saying that no man can own a wild animal. I've always agreed with this but it's a bit different if you poach from a game farm or stocked trout lake which have been developed by man. He also would tell me he wasn't a poacher because he had never been prosecuted!

Poaching has always been with me and around me. I've grown up with it, maybe through some of the thoughts and approaches of Bernie who taught me how to tickle trout, net salmon and also a little bit of his know-how about boats. The Indian canoe I use on the Pond was a gift from Bernie and I've just acquired another of his boats, a small, traditionally-lined rowing boat with an old Seagull outboard engine. I'm going to use this on the estuary. Both of these boats were handmade by Bernie and I like to think, when I'm sitting in them, that maybe a little piece of his spirit or his good luck sails with me, helping me to find that bigger fish!

I've not only learned my poaching from others. Like with ordinary fishing, it is something that I've had to learn by trial and error and I learnt the art from a very early age. To date, I've never joined the angling club or bought a day ticket for the Pond. When I first started to fish, anglers used to ask me if I had a ticket and if not, why not, and I shouldn't be fishing without one. But now all the club members know me and I know them. In fact I do more for the Pond than most of the club members. I'm always cleaning up rubbish, clearing weed which spreads like wildfire in the summer, and looking after the general maintenance and well being of the pond. I believe also that I care and love the Pond far more than anybody from the club. I proposed to my loved one in my Indian canoe in the middle of the pond (and it was on one knee, which takes a great deal of skill, especially when holding a diamond ring!).

I believe poaching and angling is in all of us, every man and woman on the earth. Fishing is a hunting spirit and poaching is just going that little bit further back to the roots of all human existence. When I poach, I reach a frame of mind that sets my sights on one thing: all my energy and emotion focuses on catching a fish.

8 |

It's a strange day. I hadn't planned to go fishing, yet here I am. When you live as close to a pond as I do, this often happens. Each time I see a carp move, surface or feed, I run home, grab my nearest available tackle and then run back to try to catch it. Today it's not carp but roach and rudd.

My youngest brother and two or three of his friends have been fishing since early this morning and have only caught a couple of roach. It is now the afternoon and their patience is running low. They are beginning to argue and shout at each other, and now one of them has caught his float up a tree! I can see the branch where it is caught shake and tremble as the small boy climbs to try to retrieve his precious float. With a snap, the branch springs back into place, from which now the float loaded with shot is gently swinging. His line has snapped, causing a great uproar from the boys. Some are laughing and others shouting and the familiar words are said, 'I'll have to set up again!'

I've decided to leave them to it, and walking away I look behind the reeds. A few days ago there was a heavy downpour which caused the Pond to rise a good foot or more. At one end of the Pond there are reeds, which cover about half an acre of water two feet deep. The angling club has put corrugated iron a little way into the reeds to stop fish from escaping but with all the rain we've had lately, water has risen above the iron and I've noticed that many carp have escaped to the other side. Every so often I can see the reeds knock in a very forceful way, indicating that the carp are there.

I climb a tree that looks over the reeds. With my polarized sun glasses, which take the surface glare off the water, I look into a clear opening in the reeds which spread out about ten feet from the bank. I can't see my carp but there is a very large shoal of roach and rudd.

As soon as I see them I jump out of the tree, run home, get a rod, reel, float and enough shot to weigh it down, a packet of hooks and a disgorger. On the way back to the reeds I stop to get some maggots from my brother and continue to my spot by the reeds to set up. I am using a small stick float and a size eighteen hook. The bank where I had seen the shoal is covered in trees and bushes – a small hawthorn bush and many small ash trees border the reeds. I try to slide the rod through the mass of twigs and branches, but I am soon caught and tangled. I try again, this time the float is free. I swing my float like a pendulum to get some distance in my cast, let go of my line and it drops in the middle of the opening. It lands with such a splash the roach disappear in a split second.

I reel in a bit and then try to re-cast, but the wind is blowing and I am tangled up in an ash tree, I pull down and reel in completely. What I need is . . . I look around, behind and to the right of me is covered in bamboo – perfect! I cut down the longest cane I can find, which is about thirteen feet long, strip it of all its foliage, tie a hook length on of about three feet and then bait up with two maggots. I push my pole out in the opening and into the fish, my free-lined maggots begin to fall, a fish takes it straight away and I strike it. The bamboo bends double as I bring in a four ounce rudd. I unhook it and take it to my brother's keepnet. 'He's got one,' they all say in unison as I hurriedly put the fish into the net and run back to the reeds two or three swims down.

I put the pole back into the opening and as soon as the maggot starts to sink, a fish grabs at it. I bring it to the bank, unhook it and take it to the keepnet.

'He's caught more in half an hour than we've caught all day,' grumbles one of Toby's friends. This carries on for about six fish until Toby and one of his friends follow me back to where I am fishing. They snigger at my rather odd and primitive contraption, but when I catch another fish, their smirks turn to frowns of disbelief. I disgorge the fish and give it to Toby to put in the keepnet.

I can hear the cuckoo. It's the first time I've heard it this year and it's quite early. A little time has passed since I caught my last fish as the shoal moved away, but it has now come back and I move my bamboo pole slowly towards them. I watch four fish all go for the maggots, stop and nudge the bait with their snouts. One takes it and I pull it in. As I walk into the swim where my brother and his friends are fishing I stop short. All four of them are using bits of bamboo cane, their modern rods and reels thrown aside. It reminds me of photographs I have seen of Chinese fishermen, all lined up, cramped together using huge poles.

I put my fish in the keepnet and leave them to it. I'm returning to catch some more fish, this time with a very pleased expression on my face!

9|

I'm sitting in the shade of a wide oak tree on a steep bank on the south side of the Pond. It is a perfect midsummer's day. Earlier this morning I caught a nice leather carp of about seventeen pounds. After the flurry of emotions of playing it very close to snags and weeds, I've decided to rest for a while, contemplate and write a little.

From where I am sitting I can see about seven or eight carp all lying on the surface, resting and basking in the morning sunshine. They've placed themselves in small pockets of Canadian pond weed that has suddenly grown over the last few weeks of hot weather. It almost covers the surface of the pond and it is very thick and dense in some places. Personally I don't really mind the weed. It makes the pond a bit more interesting – the carp are now in places they would usually never like to be and it gives them a little more confidence – but most of all I like the weed problem because it keeps the other fishermen away! The carp anglers don't like their rigs tangled and match anglers don't like losing their floats.

The only problem weed creates for me is trying to paddle through it in my canoe when I am looking for lost tackle – which I might add is very enjoyable. I've done this ever since I can remember, collecting floats and bomb weights which are usually out of reach to anyone standing on the bank, dredging for rigs and bombs from the bottom by scraping the floor of the Pond with a large bamboo cane. The list of my tackle finds is endless, even large items of tackle have been found which fishermen have left after night sessions: landing nets, keepnets and sacks, rod rests and only the other day I found a brand new stainless-steel rod pod. To date I haven't found a rod or reel, but I live in hope!

The largest number of floats I've found in one day is sixteen and after a good dredging session I went home with twelve bomb weights. Nearly all the tackle I find I keep or give to my brothers Jonjo and Toby. Some I return to the rightful owners if they tell me what they've lost.

A carp has just jumped clean out of the water causing waves to spread out to the bank. I thought the carp would have had enough of splashing around after the excellent performance they put on a few weeks ago when they were spawning. The sight of carp spawning is an incredible one. I sat for hours watching the carp which were as close as two inches from the bank. I could actually touch them with my hands. Their fear of humans is completely forgotten when they set to the task of procreation.

I can also see a large shoal of rudd sunbathing. I was talking to a matchman yesterday who organizes matches here every Wednesday night. He was in a despondent mood as the winners of the matches were only catching fish of weights up to about two pounds. In fact one of the matchmen tried resorting to catching carp, but with little success. He blames the weed growth for the lack of form.

In fact, Trevor, the matchman, is here today. He's over at the Blown-up pond behind this bigger one. He's hired a little digger and is taking the silt away from an overflow, which in turn will help to stop the bigger pond from silting up. One of the problems of these old estate ponds is that the water level is getting lower because of the silt and run-off from the fields and also because the old drainage systems aren't allowing the silt to flow out of the ponds into the river. I did go over and offer to help but there wasn't anything I could do.

From where I am sitting I can see across the Pond and into the distance. There is a beautiful blue field of linseed which reflects and radiates the sky, contrasting with a cornfield and pasture along its sides. The linseed is almost a grey-blue which makes the sky seem very light in comparison.

I've been away for a couple of weeks on holiday, sunning myself, eating, drinking and snorkelling. The fish in distant countries are certainly very different from any I see at home. While I was snorkelling a very large octopus rose from the depths, turned blue and came at me. It was one of the most frightening things that has ever happened to me.

When I got back from holiday the air was full of new developments. A dual carriageway is going to be built a few miles away, tearing up and cutting into the beautiful Cornish countryside. The suggested routes were released showing where the new bridge over the River Tamar is to be sited. One of the routes was just a few yards from where I live but I'm glad to see that this area has been designated a place of special environmental importance and the cost would anyway have been too much. I am sure that if it was not so expensive to build here they would have gone ahead, as it seems that the County Council doesn't care about the countryside at all.

The route they have decided on rips up some of the most beautiful hedgerow and hillside, almost destroying rural life in this part of Cornwall just to fulfil the need of holidaymakers. It seems nowadays that all of Cornwall is geared to the holiday season. Even rural life! Farms are turning into barn conversions and holiday flats, camping sites, bed and breakfast houses, swimming pools and chalets and Cornwall's glorious past of fishing and tin mining has been forgotten. Far too many of our villages and small coastal ports and harbours have become commercialized, with amusement parks, ice-cream parlours and souvenir shops selling rock and 'I love Cornwall' T-shirts. If you visited these places in the dead of winter, you would be forgiven for thinking you were in 'ghost towns'. Shops are boarded up and all the owners are away in the South of France for the winter. Only the sight of local fishermen mending their nets will give a clue to what the place used to be like.

What changes the fishermen have seen! Even the fishing regulations have changed since we joined the EC, and not for the better either.

I sometimes go for a walk on Dartmoor. It's wonderful to walk for miles and miles following rivers and tors and not seeing another human being at all.

Actually, here on the Pond there's no one around today and it's a Friday. I mustn't speak too soon, since it's only half past twelve!

It wouldn't surprise me one bit to see somebody later camping out over the weekend.

A heron has just landed on the opposite bank. I keep meaning to get a photograph of him, but whenever I bring my camera out he has either disappeared or is just not around.

Since I started writing today, the sun has moved and the carp have moved with it, so I think it's about time that I go fishing again and try to outwit another one!

10 |

The Blown-up pond is a very small indent of water probably only about thirty feet wide by forty feet long. In the middle there is an island that is still joined to the bank so I can walk out into the middle of it from the side, but I always refer to it as the 'island'. The banks of the Blown-up are covered and very overgrown with beeches, oaks,

bamboo, brambles and fallen down trees, so much so that there is only one pitch there. To the left of this pitch, in a corner, there is a large dead chestnut tree that has fallen into the water.

The Blown-up pond is situated behind the reeds and a little way up the valley from the larger pond. None of the anglers ever fish the smaller pond as they don't believe it holds anything, but I know different! I find it great to come here at weekends when the Pond is usually very crowded – it is a place I can escape to!

My earliest memories of the Blown-up are from when I first moved into the house by the Pond. I was about seven at the time and I remember my father showing me how to fish. We caught a monster eel and I thought how huge it was, especially as I was used to catching elvers in the small stream by our old house by lifting up stones. I can't remember catching anything else that day.

The next memory I have is why we (my brothers and I), actually call it the Blown-up pond. I remember waking up one morning to find Royal Marines invading us, running up past our house into the field where my brother keeps his pony, and over to the small pond. I didn't think much of it and carried on as normal, going to school, and I thought no more about it until I went there a few days later.

The marines had blown a hole in the dam wall causing the water to drain out. Being only about ten at the time I didn't really understand why they did it (I still don't fully . . . I suppose it was an exercise), and I still wonder to this day if they netted the fish before they blew it up. At the time, though, I didn't spare a moment's thought for the wildlife. I was too busy trying to jump from one side of the dam to the other, as boys do.

Today, all the anglers that were with the club then have moved on, so I don't think I'll ever know the true story. If I mention it to any of the new club members they look at me in disbelief. Only the other day I said to a match-man that I'd seen huge rudd over at the Blown-up and he looked at me with a frown and said 'Where's that then?', expecting it to be a pond miles away.

About two years after the marines blew up the dam, weeds grew where water once stood. A few weeks went by without me visiting it and, as if by magic, the pond was repaired to its former glory – as if it was a rusted steam train renovated and now working at full steam.

Since then the pond has slowly been restocked. I remember a couple of years ago going there and finding a whole shoal of tench, all about one to two pounds, dazed and drowsy after being stocked. I later found out that they'd been put there by mistake and should have gone into the big pond! In fact, just the other day I saw the tench spawning. It was quite strange because I was fishing for roach from the one and only pitch, half watching my float, half watching the tench, when I looked at my watch and remembered that it was time I rushed home for my tea. When I had finished and gone back to where I had left my tackle, I found, to my amazement, a dead tench! I lifted it carefully out of the water – it must have died while I was gone because it was still so very 'fresh' – I tried rubbing its heart to resuscitate her, (and even thought twice about mouth to mouth!) Its stomach was hugely inflated and resembled a balloon.

Tench, I might add, are my favourite fish, better even than the mighty carp. I love their beautiful, iridescent green scales and their stunning orange-red eyes, like a flame in a forest. After not having any luck reviving the fish I took her home with me, made a plaster cast of her, painted it, and mounted her on a beautiful piece of vintage oak.

Since the pond was blown up, many other species have been added as well as the tench, including a thirteen-pound mirror carp which somebody caught from the bigger pond and put in this one.

Not very long ago, I was fishing for tench in the Blown-up. As with the Pond in the summer the Blown-up suffers badly with Canadian pond weed, so I'd raked through the reed clearing a patch about eight feet from the bank, scattered sweetcorn fairly liberally about my cleared area, set up a light tench rod, one capable of landing a two pound fish, and waited for dark.

At dusk the mirror carp I mentioned earlier came and

started to eat my sweetcorn. I looked in disbelief, because at the time I had no idea that there was a carp in there. After a moment of horror I silently ran to my house to grab my carp rod. It was already set up so no time was wasted. I raced back to my pitch and to my joy the carp was still there, picking up corn oblivious of me. I baited a hook and then slowly and carefully cast about one yard in front of the fish. It sucked in my bait, and then spat it out again just as fast! I quietly reeled in again and cast once more, this time a little further out, and in the direction it was swimming. (I'll add at this point that the water was quite clear due to the pond weed and I had the advantage of wearing polarized sunglasses, so I could see every movement the fish made towards my hook and bait!)

The carp again picked up my bait and I struck. I felt the inevitable resistance, a solid, powerful motor, well oiled from not being caught for a while! I couldn't let much line out as it would have snagged on the fallen tree, so I used as much side pressure as I could to prevent this from happening. I was using ten pound line so I could put this pressure on, yet every so often the reel would screech as the clutch slipped. The fish fought tremendously, turning this way and then that, heading for the snags and then in the direction of the weed. Suddenly, without warning, it began to tire and slowly I began to win the battle. Closer and closer it came until it was cradled by the net.

From that day I've christened the carp Bessy, and I've

always been proud and pleased to be able to boast that I've caught the only carp in that pond. I've seen Bessy a lot since that day and I've never really been too interested in catching her again – I'm more content to see her in the water and not out! In fact, I treat her as a friend and sometimes take bait just to feed her. A carp angler spent two days and two nights at the Blown-up fishing for her with all his gadgets and techno-wizardry, but Bessy remained in the depths keeping cool and wet, the things fish love best.

Last year I climbed a tree on the island to look for Bessy and to my surprise I found a shoal of five rudd and a bream all well over a pound, the biggest being about two and a half to three pounds. I couldn't believe it! I've tried fishing for them on several occasions and found their favourite haunts. One is very close to the bank by the fallen down tree, in the left-hand corner, but somehow I haven't caught the biggest yet. For a while, after my first encounter with the big rudd, which I've called Rufus, I became almost obsessed with trying to catch him, but common sense prevailed and I always ended up catching the carp.

There are also many smaller shoals of rudd and roach which seem to disappear in the daytime and only come out at dusk. Then it's a fish a cast, but when darkness surrounds and night falls the bites fade away. This seems strange to me and I always feel a little on edge when I'm at the Blown-up. It is by nature a very dark pond because of all the leaf cover – being overgrown that it is – and when dusk comes there is a certain atmosphere which sometimes triggers emotions of fear and dread. Even in the daytime I've always got the feeling someone's looking at me.

The gamekeeper puts ducks on the Blown-up to shoot. This year there are quite a lot – I would say at a guess as many as thirty. Maybe there is a heavy atmosphere at the pond because of all the ducks that have been killed in years gone by, perhaps it's echoing and channelling the anger and pain.

Just the other day I found a yellow duckling, which is quite rare as all the other ducklings are brown and black. I looked around for its parents but I couldn't see them, so I picked it up and decided to help to look for them and crawled along the banks with the duckling in my jacket pocket. I checked everywhere, then I sat down to rest for a while and to listen for any quacks or splashes indicating ducks. I was feeling rather upset at this point. I thought I'd done the wrong thing and that I should have left the duckling alone and I had it in mind that I would take him home to rear him and let him go when he had grown up. I have kept a few ducks and chickens so I do know a little about the subject.

I thought I would take one last look around the island. To my surprise and happiness I found a duck with nine ducklings. I released the found duckling which quickly swam to the others and was accepted straight away, much to my relief.

The very next day I went back to check on the ducklings but to my disappointment and sadness seven of the ducklings had disappeared, presumably dead, including my little yellow friend.

I often think of the duckling when I'm at the Blown-up and how I should have kept him as a pet. Somebody told me once, after I witnessed the killing of a mouse by one of our pet cats, that you 'can't stop or change the instincts of an animal' and that it is 'nature's way'. But sometimes I feel that it is not fair, even in the world we live in, that the small and weak are often taken advantage of by the bigger, stronger bodies.

THE BLOWN-UP POND

The Blown-up pond is like so many other ponds and rivers, and I would even go as far as to say all ponds and rivers. They all have certain secrets that nobody knows about. Just because somebody catches a big fish they automatically think it's the largest there! I've discovered a lot of secrets about the Blown-up pond: monster rudd, big eels, Bessy, even the tench which nobody really knows about! For such a little pond to hold a three pound rudd is staggering! All this just amazes me, and I dread to think what I would find in the big pond if I knew all of its secrets.

11 |

The spirit of the night is with me. It's a different spirit to the daytime. The night spirit is cold, quiet and sinister. Night fishing is a wholly different dimension to angling. At night, hidden feelings come out: night vision, intuition and the seventh sense. That which remains hidden all day, slowly appears after dusk. At night-time it feels as if the whole world is asleep, apart from owls, water rats and voles, foxes, badgers, bats and all things nocturnal, which are only disturbed by the sound of people going home from the pub and the occasional drone of a distant car or train.

My rods are fixed in place by banksticks, all set, ready and poised for the moment of contact with a monster of the deep, a creature from a world in complete contrast to my own. I live in hope, staring at the clear night sky, watching for shooting stars or satellites, which are almost the same as a shooting star but which move at a constant rate with equal light. A feather-light summer breeze breathes all around me, the moon lightens the night.

There is an owl in a tree on the opposite bank that shrieks a call that is so ear-piercing and eerie that you could imagine it is someone being murdered, or the voice of a banshee: it is most definitely *not* the 'too-whit, too-woo' which one normally associates with owls.

Before it was dark I sat watching two squirrels fighting over a hazelnut tree. Their aerial acrobatics were amazing to see, as they leaped from tree to tree, squeaking and squawking at the top of their voices. A little while before, I also sat transfixed, looking at a kingfisher hovering in the air and then diving as fast as a bullet from a gun into the water and out again with a small roach or rudd in its beak, and then, in a blink of an eye, he'd rushed to his home on the opposite bank, peeping in his very distinctive way. I can recognize the kingfisher's call straight away. A friend of mine who is a birdwatcher, marvels at my tales of the kingfisher. He has never seen one and my answer to him is to take up angling!

I've lost count of the number of times I've seen kingfishers. Not long ago I saw two pairs fighting in what must have been a territorial battle for the Pond. In fact, the wildlife I've seen while fishing is amazing. Ponds, rivers and estuaries are abundant with life, from larger species such as herons and otters to the small rarer species like dippers and water rails, plus all the wild flowers and vegetation which only live in marshy, wet areas, and, of course, the fish. The fish themselves can be quite a spectacle – indeed, if I were very wealthy and owned a lot of land, I would let the fields turn to wild pasture, rear endangered species and endorse wild animals which, I'm sad to say, are becoming rare and endangered.

The Canadian pond weed has been the worst I can ever remember. The carp have hidden themselves away all summer, burying themselves deep down under the weeds or in small pockets in the middle. I am fishing the only 'fishable' swim on the pond. The matches finished late in July and since then the weed hasn't been raked out – the matchmen usually do it! Even now I've cast my rods out and am hoping their baits haven't snagged on weeds, because even if the water looks clear it's usually only because the weed hasn't reached the top. At the moment, even I am looking forward to the weed dying back as the carp fishing has become rather slow! I haven't caught a decent sized carp for over a month because they are preoccupied with the food found in the weed and not in the fishermen's bait.

Due to the match fishermen not raking out the weed, the Pond is now in the clutch of a vicious cycle. The regular anglers are keeping away because of the weed, and because the pond is not being fished, the weed is growing ever thicker, which will keep the anglers away longer, and so on and so on until it will be impossible to fish at all! Perhaps the Pond will fish better in the autumn and winter months when the weed will slowly die back. Usually around this time and until the beginning of spring, carp fishing is very difficult and nobody, except the locals, catch anything. The carp hide themselves away deep in the reeds, perhaps getting some sort of warmth from the roots, but also eating bloodworm which collect there.

Right now it's coming to the end of summer and the reeds are still a deep green, not the browns and rusts of autumn and winter. The temperature tonight is as high as it will be on an October day. In fact, my sleeping bag has its zip undone and I am not wearing my jumper as I usually would. In fact, it's so warm I think it may entice the carp to feed a little more.

A rat – or water vole as I always call them – as big as a small cat has just run underneath my rod and rests. I don't really mind them – watching them and the surroundings helps me to pass the time until a carp decides to go for my bait. There are quite a lot of rats here on the Pond, encouraged by the amount of litter left by the anglers.

My silver foil bite alarm has just lifted a small way – is it a line bite? The moment of sheer anxiety is on me. Do I strike, which will connect me with a current of electricity exciting my every movement, or should I wait for something more positive – a run with such power that line gushes from my reel causing acceleration and a burst of energy exploding into a battle that only dreams are made of? I decide to wait for something a bit more positive to happen, because I am now sure that if I strike now, I will be left reeling in my bait and trying to re-cast my line in the dark in a very weedy patch of water.

I actually took my hooks, baits and lines out on my Indian canoe so I could be sure of fishing in a weed-free patch. I then scattered my offerings to the spirit of the Pond and the carp. My bait and offerings are part modern and part traditional. I am using maple-flavoured beans, including blackeye, kidney and butterbeans, and sweetcorn, all of which have been cooked for about an hour and then soaked in sugared water for a number of weeks. Now they have fermented and there is a deep layer of scum on the top, which is an added attraction for the carp. The angler has to go to the trouble of cooking beans and nuts (peanuts, tigernuts etc.) because if they aren't cooked they will absorb moisture from the fish, swell up and kill the fish. Last season a large carp on the Pond died. The secretary of the club, who is also a split-cane user – but he uses them as if they are modern carp rods, an identical pair of rods and reels – took the dead carp for an autopsy and was told that a swollen uncooked nut was the cause of death.

It is now just past one a.m. and I'm starting to feel drowsy. I fall asleep for a moment or two and then the spirit of the Pond wakes me. It gives me a little nudge every so often to remind me to watch my rods. The stars have moved a fraction since I last looked at them, or have I moved?

I'm beginning to wonder if my bait is going to work. Should I have a worm rod out, and try for a big eel? Then the night wouldn't seem so long, because I would be bound to catch an eel!

Suddenly, without any warning, my silver foil bite alarm bounces up and hits the underneath of my rod, and line runs free from my reel. Without hesitation I struggle from the sleeping bag. Once out, I pull up hard on my rod and click the bale arm over on my reel. My clutch then sounds as I feel the mighty force that is a carp. Out of the darkness I can hear the sound of a carp trying to break free and get back to his peaceful existence underwater. The sound of splashing breaks the silence of the clear night, and ripples spread across the moonlit pond. I reel in and start to retrieve line taken by its initial run, turning the fish towards me as it tries to swim with force and momentum in the reeds to my left. My rod arches over, pointing at the reeds as I try to pull the fish from the direction it is heading. The carp's head is finally turned and he starts to tire as I increase the pressure and tighten my clutch. The fish is now only yards away from the bank as I reach behind me in search of my landing net. I slowly and gently sink the old net into the water so as not to scare the fish. Now he is nearer I can see that I have played the fish through a lot of weed. I gently pull him over the net and raise it, catching the fish. I put him gently down onto the grass which is covered by my weigh sling, rest my rod on the bank and switch on my small pencil torch which gives me my first view of the fish. It is a large common carp, its beautiful golden scales reflecting the beam of the torch. Its magical eye, which matches the colour of his scales, is staring at me. I wonder if he can see me? Probably the brightness of the light is blinding him. The hook is just in his upper lip and is quickly removed. The weigh sling is pulled up around him then slowly pulled from the ground, the spring balance is set and now I can see that magical number which will either delight or dishearten. The scales stretch, up and up they go, past eight, nine, ten, and finally settling at eighteen and three-quarter pounds, a marvellous carp. I much prefer commons to mirror carp. They are so much prettier, but probably also because here in the Pond mirrors outnumber commons by four to one. If it was the other way, perhaps I'd prefer mirrors!

I return the magical common to the dark watery depths, the ripples float into blackness.

THE NIGHT~TIME

The night drifts by effortlessly and the carp fisher can rest with peace of mind, without fear of paranoia due to not catching a carp. Not landing a fish is very disheartening — it's better not to have played and lost than never to have played at all. A sense of confusion begins in the carp fisher if days and nights go by without landing a fish. Is the bait wrong, is the weather too hot or too cold, too windy, not windy enough, am I losing my touch, are there any carp in here? A lack of confidence begins to pervade him and there seems to be no light at the end of the tunnel. Periods like these haunt the carp fisher. What tends to happen with me is that after a barren spell I usually catch a lot of fish all at once or over a few days. Weeks and months go by without a carp, and then I am catching them like there is no tomorrow.

Sometimes, if I haven't caught a carp for a while, I blame it on other things. Perhaps I've been too busy catching roach or tench or another species, or I've been doing something called 'work' which must be done every now and then to stop people moaning at me and to pay the vintage tackle dealers whom I constantly phone for new 'old' rods and reels and other bits and pieces.

I've just been sleeping. It was a very light sleep and it feels like it only lasted a minute. But now I'm awake I can see that dawn surrounds me, so I must have slept for at least four hours. My bite indicator is still on the floor, so it seems that I've had no more bites. Trying not to break the stillness of a new day, I silently reel in my rod, only to find my bait missing! Did I have a run when I was asleep? I decide that I must have done. I don't feel that I will catch another fish – I can see that it's going to be a hot day and I am sure that the carp will be at the other end of the pond parading in the late summer sun.

12 |

The dawn mist surrounds me as I write, a cold, fresh beginning to a new day. I always find the dawn a fabulous part of the day, one minute deafening silence, the next ear-piercingly noisy as the birds begin their dawn chorus.

I am sitting in a pitch which is very close to the reeds and a carp is moving. It started to feed and bubble earlier as it churned up the bottom for bloodworms and other such delicacies and I slowly and precisely cast a large lob worm in its direction. Now I'm waiting!

The sun starts to rise making the mist appear thicker as it mixes and condenses with the cold air. For some reason the birds have stopped singing, making me feel uneasy. It is at times like this that I am suddenly aware of the spirit of the Pond; not some ghost, spectre or apparition, but an actual power. I am often aware of it.

Sometimes it's happy, other times, like now, it's sombre, even frightening and scary. It's a power that appears to determine whether I'm going to catch a fish or no; the very source and heart of the Pond. It's very spiritual, and connects itself to something deep within me — almost as if we talk and converse with each other.

Perhaps today 'the spirit' has made me uneasy because I'm fishing in the wrong spot and there're huge shoals of carp a few yards down the bank just waiting to be caught, or maybe I've done something wrong and offended it in some way. Quite often I start to do something and then stop myself half-way through thinking the spirit wouldn't like it, that it won't reward my patience by letting me catch a fish if I carry on. I often think about this when I'm about to embark on a particular way of fishing that perhaps I shouldn't, like stalking a carp from a tree. On the other hand, I've found I can use the spirit to my own advantage. I've often undone some other fisherman's thoughtlessness, more often than not cleaning up their litter which is always a major problem. Some anglers think 'I've done my fishing, I can't be bothered to take it home'. The worst, however, is when anglers discard rubbish in the nearest hedge or bush, I suppose thinking 'out of sight out of mind'. But this is not the case. As soon as autumn and winter approach, the leaves die back leaving an array of convicting evidence: rusted sweetcorn and luncheon-meat cans, polythene bags, crisp packets and, worst of all, camping gas canisters!

After performing my 'good deeds' I partake in an intelligent conversation with the trees, the water, the weeds and reeds, the friendly robin and anything else around the Pond that is an expression of the spirit, telling them all what I've done, and hopefully shifting the dreaded curse of not catching a fish onto the shoulders of the 'offenders'. Perhaps there'll be a reward for my efforts, maybe some gold in the shape of a carp!

Another good thing to get on the right side of the pond spirit is to reverse damage other people have done, such as anglers who have ripped branches off trees just to cast a few yards further. I go along afterwards and try to repair the deformation. A while ago someone started attacking the Blown-up pond by trying to build some sort of a new pitch using old railway sleepers, so I, to add a few gold stars to my name in the good books of the spirit, threw them off the dam wall, never to be seen again. Later that week I stalked out the only carp in the Blown-up so I must have impressed the spirit no end! That same day, however, I did talk to a match angler who was distraught by the disappearance of his sleepers. Of course my reply was that I knew nothing about the matter and it probably involved some young hooligans.

Over the years the Pond's spirit has physically worked its way into my body, via cuts from falling out of trees, scratches from brambles, stings from midges, and I have even drunk and swallowed the water, which has slowly filtered through my body and drained into my soul. As I fish I am gradually becoming saturated and camouflaged by my surroundings, by the pond. I feel as if I am part of it, and it is part of me. A day doesn't pass without me being here, fishing, walking, looking, talking, smelling, floating in every inch of grassed bank and rippled bay. If I'm not here I'm bound to be thinking about it, wishing I was. I suppose a part of me is always here, sitting in favourite swims, casting for that elusive carp or golden rudd.

When I visit other waters for pike, tench and other species, I never feel the same as when I'm fishing here. The spirits in other ponds hide themselves away from me, and I only feel a slight presence.

I remember once fishing in a very over-populated pool. I was catching carp by the bucket-full, the biggest being about sixteen pounds and the smallest under a pound, but the fish were in a terrible condition with ripped lips, carp pox, missing scales and torn fins. The spirit of that pond was screaming in pain and anger, an atmosphere heavy with cries of fish which scared me and I made sure I would never return to fish it again. It's been shut down now I'm glad to hear.

On other ponds the spirit is as wary of me as I am of it – we are strangers. Sometimes it rewards me and I start to feel we are friends. Another time we can be enemies fighting each other, which usually results in a missed fish, a snap, a tangle or, worst of all, the hook slipping just as the fish is about five feet from the bank and ready to land. Feelings of frustration and sorrow weigh upon me at times like this — I can't even blame myself for not tying a hook on correctly or not fishing with strong enough line. The only thing I do blame is the spirit. The anger wells up deep inside me and I can hear and feel the whole pond laughing at me. This, in turn, drives me further and deeper into the quest of finding and catching the fish I'm after to prove the spirit wrong and to beat it at its own game.

But here at the Pond the spirit and I are on much more sociable terms, although as in all relationships there are ups and downs — like catching a twenty pound carp and suffering snapped tips, or catching a two pound roach and having to put up with line getting tangled while casting from a centre pin — but on the whole we are the best of friends.

The sun is now slowly creeping around the Pond, waking new life, beckoning them to show themselves to a new day. The spirit is still with me and has slowly warmed me up, making me feel comfortable again and at ease with myself and my surroundings. I'm not uneasy as I was before.

The line on my rod has just started to twitch and within what seems a millionth of a second has become taut and has begun to peel off my reel – a run! I pull up hard on my rod feeling the electricity rushing through the line connecting me with an unseen water world. The fish dives deep and heads straight towards the reeds. Side strain is needed. My old cane rod creaks and cries out to be locked up in a glass-fronted cabinet and just admired and looked at by passers-by. Even my reel shrieks to be taken home and to be treated nicely and with a little respect. I force the carp to head in the opposite direction. The power of the fish can only be equalled and compared to a train running on full steam. The spirit *was* telling me something earlier ... to be ready; it gave me a fright to make me more aware of what was going on around me.

I slowly and surely gain and gather line, and at every inch of line gained my reel and rod moan. The Canadian pond weed slows my retrieval and tires the fish.

Just as the carp is getting close to the bank it takes off with one last attempt to escape. The thought of the spirit is on my mind. Is it with me or is it going to be evil and let me down at the last second and then laugh at me as it's done so many times before?

The fish gets closer and closer. I dip my ancient landing net into the water and increase the pressure to lift the fish's head out over the front of the net. Splashes ripple around the pond, waking moorhens and ducks, the quiet dawn after the morning chorus erupts into life and in the centre of this microcosm, a fish, a life and water!

THE SPIRIT OF THE POND

I raise my net and place it on the bank. A carp, its beautiful golden eye looking, staring at me as if in wonder, in thought. Two aliens from different worlds marvel at each other, comparing lives.

The pleasantries are over, the initial weigh, a little under twenty pounds, a photograph or two, and we bid each other a fond farewell. He shakes my hand and I shake his fin and then slowly and carefully

I release his marvellous figure back into his own world, one of swan mussels, weed, bloodworms, silt, reeds, and fallen down trees. I think of my world: cars, concrete, developments. I know which I'd prefer!

The carp lies in the shallows for a moment, his gills readjust to the water and then with a gentle flick of the tail he is away back into the depths of the Pond. The spirit was with me today!

Now that I've been successful, the spirit melts away until the next time I want to catch a fish, when it will return either to be a help or a hindrance. Today is the same as many others — when I've caught one fish and because I live so close to the Pond my appetite for angling deserts me and I pack up to go home. As I leave I thank the spirit of the Pond for helping me out, and just to keep on good terms with it I throw in some left-over stale bread which I found in the bottom of my bag to feed the ducks. Only then can I wander away and return to my house, leaving the spirit to exercise its wrath on some other poor angler.

13|

The golden colours
of autumn bathe
the Pond in that
wonderful light which
is only associated with
this time of year. Long shadows throw light and shade on
areas that aren't usually transformed in this way. The
Canadian pond weed is starting to turn a light rust colour,
the start of its decaying process. When there is weed on
the pond it is always hard to imagine what it's like not to
have it, and vice versa. Earlier I was in my Indian canoe
and I thought how hard it was to steer and row through
the weed, and I tried to remember how the Pond was
before the weed grew, but I couldn't.

Today my fishing is for that scavenging fish the perch,

which I can only compare to a crow. I find the best bait for perch are worms. I can remember once stalking a carp from underneath a overhanging bush. I had been waiting from sunrise until midday for that elusive carp, my worm cast correctly into the perfect place. It was just a matter of time before a monster from the deep decided to steer. Then, from out of nowhere, my line started to twitch and my rod tip to skate as if it was nervous about catching a carp of supreme size. Instead of this, when I struck, I found not the almighty rush and reel-screaming fight, but a feeble 'jagged' fight as I landed a half pound perch. I was more shocked than surprised as this small fellow had swallowed my size-four hook plus two large lobworms! Indeed there has been many a time when I've been fishing for carp with worms and have caught other fish.

Once I was fishing, again for carp. My bait was a rod's length away from me and the water was quite clear so I could see my bait and anything that happened to it. I could see an eel gently swimming around and I knew immediately that it was about to take my bait, and it did! But the strange thing was that it hooked itself before it touched my worms.

I've always associated autumn with perch and pike. For my pike fishing I travel to Slapton near Dartmouth in Devon. It's a good hour and a half's drive from where I live but there is nowhere closer. Somebody told me once that pike were banned from Cornwall! I'm not sure if this

THE AUTUMN PERCH

is true, but I've still to find a pond with pike in it in this area. And as this book is about my beloved ponds, I will leave pike to another time and place!

I often find perch bite better around and a little after dusk – the big ones that is! I've groundbaited an area with casters, chopped worms and some bran which I usually find helps the proceedings along. My rod is an eleven-foot Avon with four pound line, teamed with a Grice and Youngs Avon Supreme centre pin. My bite indicator is a very fine traditional perch bobber which is cocked with three AA shots and a size twelve hook baited with two halves of a chopped worm.

My pretty orange-tipped float lightens the green murky water wonderfully, occasionally sinking and disappearing to show that a fish is attached. Watching a float for hours at a time mesmerizes me, making me more and more addicted to angling. As I sit taking in the surroundings and breathing in the pond's scents I am reminded of past times. For example, the smell of crushed water celery reminds me of eel catching in small streams when I was young, and the stench of maggots turning to casters always takes me back to roach fishing one summer holiday when life was less hectic and worries of going back to school were the last thing on my mind.

I'm catching more rudd than perch – they're biting very intently and I don't have to wait long for the next one, but there are now a few spots of rain starting to fall and the sky is not so bright as it was earlier, so I think I'll put my brolly up.

I am now under the umbrella, the rain is heavier and larger drops of water are falling from the trees above my swim, making loud noises as they hit the brolly. Fishing

in the rain makes me feel cosy and snug inside my little shelter, it also reminds me of camping in tents by seaside towns as it always seems to rain whenever you decide to go camping. Although I never seem to catch much when the rain is very heavy – it seems to put the fish off feeding – I'm still getting the odd bite or two.

The shower has now passed and with the rain stopping, a stronger, more positive bite is occurring. My float bobs under and then rises to the surface, and again as if the fish is unsure about taking it. But patience is the key to all fishing especially when it comes to float fishing. Now my float has vanished completely and I strike, feeling the fish on the other end. My rod bends into what seems to be a good-sized fish as it kites one way and then the other. As it comes closer I can see that it's a perch, the dorsal fin sailing through the water pretending to be an ancient galleon, its stripey green back and that fierce face staring at me as I slip my landing net underneath it and raise it on to the bank.

When my brother first started fishing, he would always tell me how he had read that the fins on a perch were poisonous if they stabbed you. Like a fool, I believed him! I always think of him when I'm unhooking a perch as the sharp spines always seem to stick into me! This perch weighs a little under two pounds, which isn't a monster as perch go, but I'm pleased with it and indeed it is a very good size perch for the Pond!

I can remember that the Pond once had far more perch in it than it has now. I think the first fish I ever caught from here was a small perch and so was the first fish my brother Jonjo caught.

A former secretary of the club explained to me once that perch have population explosions and then seem to die off afterwards. These explosions are due to the weather, he said. But there are very few perch in the Pond now and in some ways this is quite good for the ones which are left, because they are all of medium to large size.

Rudd are plentiful in the Pond. The Pond's claim to fame is that it was featured in the *Angling Mail* year book of 1981, showing some match anglers after the 'golden rudd' which still inhabit the Pond – this of course was before the carp boom. Now, nearly all the anglers who fish on the Pond are carp anglers. They forget the beautiful rudd, roach, perch, tench and gudgeon as they go about their business casting two-ounce leads about the Pond.

However, I am happy with my catch today. Nothing huge or of massive weight, but still a good day's fishing!

SPIRITUAL FISHING

14 |

Angling intuition is something I've always been interested in and as an angler have sometimes felt: sometimes not knowingly, other times quite strongly. What makes me think of this is something that happened the other day.

Somebody came to visit our house and I wasn't in a sociable mood. I felt the urge to go fishing – not just the feeling of excitement every angler feels, but a strong pulling sensation almost as if the Pond was calling to me. In fact, as I rushed out of the house holding two slices of bread, my rod, reel, landing net and a few other bits and pieces, I said to my loved one that I could hear a carp.

I ran down to the Pond, and flicked a piece of bread flake under a tree where I knew there might be carp. I waited for a while and then slowly and carefully crept around under another overhanging tree. I could see a carp move in the swim, so I cast with an underhand flick about a yard in front of it in the direction that it was swimming. The flake was free-lined, so it slowly sank leaving a trail of scent and crumbs. The carp drifted closer to the bait and hesitantly watched, then raised his head and swallowed. A quick, sharp-reactioned strike and I felt that hard living wall which is a carp! I was fishing in a very confined swim and snags were on either side of me. I had my clutch tightened right up to stop the run of line – I was using ten-pound line and I felt it wouldn't snap under such immense pressure. The carp swam this way and that as if I'd angered it and it raged to get free. I hoped and prayed the hook wouldn't slip or the line snap, causing feelings of sorrow and frustration. But these feelings weren't to be, as I slid my landing net under its golden flanks and saw a beautiful common carp surrounded in mesh. It weighed a little over eighteen pounds, and I think it was one I'd caught before when it was a pound lighter!

You might think this was coincidence, but I know it wasn't. Sometimes I'm not aware of this 'inner consciousness' until I've caught a fish; and then, when the fish is in the landing net I have a feeling of déjà-vu, as if I knew I was going to catch that fish. I often reminisce while fishing, trying to remember if I initially felt that inevitable pull; and therefore what tactics my instincts forced me to use. Indeed, quite often I find I've fished with more concentration, subconsciously communicating, stalking and hunting the intended fish.

I believe that power, sensitivity and a hidden confidence can make or break a fisherman and their intended quarry. I've met many anxious anglers, worried about being in the right place, using the right bait and the most suitable tackle. This lack of confidence at the beginning of a day's or a week's fishing often leads to a fishless trip.

The angler's intuition, however, can also be swings and roundabouts. As well as a magnetism that pulls me towards the Pond, there is also often a repulsion, something that tells me not to bother setting up my rods as I won't be catching anything today. When this happens I usually take no notice of my feelings and go ahead and fish, finding myself catching nothing and my inner voice laughing at me. Still, as every good angler knows, being there is more than enough. I am sure that a keen angler sees more wildlife than most environmentalists, because ponds, rivers and lakes are such natural wildlife havens. The angler spends so much time watching, looking and waiting that he dissolves into the landscape and can hear such things as the subliminal call of creatures like the big carp.

The fisherman watches the seasons come and go. From newly-sprouted buds to the heat of summer and on to the bronzes of autumn and the cold of winter. When I fish I take in all that surrounds me, noticing such things as an early summer, the first cuckoo and other such wonderful sights and sounds. An old Chinese poet or philosopher once said something on the lines of . . . 'to fish with a hook would ruin my fishing!' I feel this way when I am privileged to be fishing by the waterside and a robin feeds by my feet or a kingfisher dives for his supper a stone's throw away.

Spiritual fishing might be a different world away from a match angler on a canal, but the elements of all angling, be it coarse, game or sea, remain the same. After all, the matchman and specimen hunter's aim at the end of the day is to catch fish. Angling intuition, insight and knowledge of the water will all help the angler to a good day's fishing.

15 |

The Pond lies brown and gold in water-soaked fields, mud tracks and leafless trees. Water pours over the dam and, like a mini Niagara Falls, it fills the field between the Pond and the estuary.

I have never known a winter like it! Cornish winters are usually damp and mild, rarely extremely cold; but this year has been especially chilly and wet. Widespread flooding has caused major disruption in towns and on the roads. Coastal ports and ancient fishing villages are all counting the cost.

Not a carp has been caught by any of the regulars for ages. The weed has died down but in places it remains as thick as ever, the fish hiding away waiting for the warm sunny days to come around again so they can parade in all their glory along the reeds and weed beds. Today is the first sunny day we have had for weeks. It's wonderful to feel the warm sun on my face as I write, although I'm sure it won't last long.

A strange and sad thing happened to me a few weeks ago. Since I first wrote about the Blown-up pond another carp has been added, a twenty pound common carp which appeared to have a bad back. The carp, which I saw a lot with Bessy, appeared to be very dark in colour and I christened him 'Blacky'. For months I tried to catch Blacky so that I could once again say that I'd caught every carp in the Blown-up pond, but being a big, wise old carp, he remained uncaught. Although I had managed to get Bessy to feed, I couldn't get Blacky to feed as well, until one day a few weeks ago when for a change I moved my Indian canoe from the Pond to the Blown-up, where the water was crystal clear. Paul Taylor, a fishing friend and I were rowing around, looking down into the water searching for carp when after a while I found Blacky in amongst some weed on the bed. Without hesitation, I made a mental map of where he was and rowed to the bank and ran home for my tackle. I was soon back in my boat over the spot where I'd seen Blacky. I lowered a hook baited with bread flake in front of his mouth. My canoe being twelve feet long is quite susceptible to wind and this particular day was quite breezy, so we had a struggle to keep the canoe in the same place to make sure the bait was not affected. Suddenly Blacky fell for the trap, I saw my bait disappear and I soon

struck up on my rod. The line began to tighten and the carp headed for the nearest snagg. Playing fish in boats is a totally different experience from playing from the bank; quite often I find myself being towed along as there is no anchor or drogue on my canoe. After the initial run the battle between man and nature had begun. I then began to win as I brought a landing net up from the depths filled with golden light and success. I struggled my way to the bank where we stood in awe of such a beautiful fish: scales perfect, supreme size (over twenty pounds), a classic shape and line and with a large and powerful tail fin. A quick photo and then the goodbye as he splashed to go free.

I can hear you say this isn't a sad story, but I haven't finished yet! A week after this epic fight a wind blew up bringing a violent gale and storm and a large tree fell into the Blown-up pond almost covering half the surface.

When the water ran clear again, I once again rowed my canoe to the middle to look for watery life. I found Blacky at the same spot as when I'd last seen him, but I could see patches of white on his tail and back. I gently knocked him with my paddle. Any healthy fish would have swam away at great speed, but Blacky looked ill. My tackle was in the boat so I gently dipped my landing net under the water and down to where Blacky lay, then raised the net up bringing him with it. Blacky didn't move the whole time. No 'great fight'. He was a sad fish. When I got him to the bank I saw to my horror that he had no tail left, it was just a stump, scales were missing along his back and tail and his dorsal fin was ripped to shreds.

The sight of Blacky saddened me greatly and would sadden any fisherman, carper or not. I showed other fishermen and friends – some said it was fin rot but I can't see how this would happen in just one week! Some people said it was perch attacking an unwell fish, but I believe it was the tree that had fallen into the water. I think Blacky got trapped underneath it and ripped his tail fin and dorsal trying to escape the branches and twigs. To see Blacky trying to swim now is heartbreaking. He rocks from side to side, not the effortless glide of before.

Blacky was my last carp of the old season. As I said before, with there being no close season, my fishing begins and ends on the first of January.

In the New Year, I look back at a year's fishing and try and break old records and personal bests, set either in the last year or from many years ago. Also it's a time to set new targets and to go to new ponds and rivers and try to complete old ambitions which never seem to come about. But ever since the New Year, there has been nothing but rain and disastrous floods. Unused Christmas presents wait patiently for the day when old favourites will be left behind, their days numbered.

My loved one and her non-fishing friends and family can never understand fully why I need so many different rods and reels. They can't appreciate that separate rods and reels have their different uses, like float rods for roach fishing, Mark IV's for carp and pike, centre pins for rivers, fixed spools for . . . and so on.

I could fish and live with just one rod if I fished for one species alone, but I don't! I could possibly get away with using a Mark IV Avon for most of my angling life, but this rod would be quite inadequate

THE WORST OF WINTER

for close range stalking in snaggs and up trees, in weed and reeds, so I must have a choice.

January and February in Cornwall are my least favourite months of the year. They're always wet, bleak and un-inspiring. October and November, if dry, are wonderful with trees bronzed and golden, reflecting the autumn sunlight; December is the advent to Christmas, which is excitement in expectations, something to look forward to. After this comes the dreaded months, nothing to look forward to, just two months of seemless rain and showers, dampness and floods. Although mild winters encourage early flowers, such as snowdrops, primroses and daffodils, these are just small sparks of light in an endless colour of greys and black.

Snow would be marvellous. It seems a lifetime ago since my last snowball fight or toboggan ride. To catch a carp in the snow . . . What a photograph that would make!

16 |

Morning sunlight gives the Pond new life. Winter floods are forgotten and suddenly spring seems to have arrived. Green buds open as if by magic. A carp breaks the surface, sending ripples across the pond, another follows, breaking the silence. I watch and listen and soon I can see one carp, two, three, four, five all following the leader. A little further out I can see three more heading across to join the main party. Today is not the first time I've ever seen carp on the surface in winter. For about the last two weeks carp have freely paraded around the middle and in one corner by the dam end and when the pond was flooded so badly and the water seemed to be 'thick' with all the run-off from the fields, the carp calmly glided on the surface.

So today, in the middle of January, my line is cast with

a floater set up. My rod is a B. James Mark IV 'Richard Walker'. It has the great man's autograph signed for all to see. I read a magazine article that said Richard Walker used to sign these rods himself, in Indian ink with a specially made pen! I like to think that a little bit of his magic and good luck has rubbed off his hand and onto the rod, causing fish to surrender under his power whenever I use it.

When I've seen carp on the surface lately, I've thrown a handful or two of dog food mixers around that area and have been quite pleased with the result. Some have been taken almost as soon as the mixer lands, others have been freely taken by the ducks!

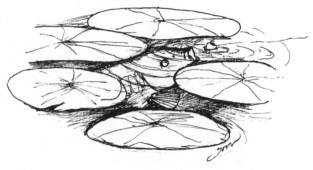

Yesterday evening I was watching the water where I'm fishing now, not expecting to see any movement. I had thrown a handful of mixers out, when a carp rose out of the water about three feet from the bank, snatched a mixer and slowly returned to its watery home. The sight made me jump and I was in a state of shock for a good while afterwards.

I was talking to an angler the other day who was interested in the history of the Pond. I have always believed it was a 'stew' pond, left over from the days of the monastery on which the main house of this grand estate was built. There was an evil monk by the name of Dando who gambled and drank far too much. The story goes that he was taken away by no less than the Devil himself, who led Dando to his death, drowned in the estuary with his dogs, in a spot which is still called Dando's Pool. There is a local legend in which it is said that Dando haunts the estate, walking its hallowed grounds. I like to think that Dando liked to fish and I often wonder if he comes back to the Pond just to keep his hand in, drinking mead or some other powerful brew.

If the Pond was a stew pond, then perhaps the carp are the forefathers of the carp here today. Thinking about it, I can compare carp to such drinks as cider, mead, ales and stout. It seems right to compare such old and beautiful creatures to something equally as old and beautiful. Some carp even have the same colouring and shades as cider and beer.

Trout, I can only compare to a light, crisp, dry white wine. The freshness of a river goes well with wine. Salmon, on the other hand, could be compared to champagne as thoughts of bubbles and spray come to mind. The pike makes me think of Irish loughs where fish have bites as hard as the whiskey. A sturgeon would be vodka from the Baltic Sea, and I would compare a tench to a full-bodied red wine, the colour of a tench's eyes; and I can see an eel would be like a dark glass of Guinness, smooth and silky.

I can't think of such comparisons for other fish, except that perhaps the chub, with its ferociousness, could be like the effects of home-made wine!

A wind has blown up and my float drifts to the left of me. I reel in and cast as far as I can, in the general direction of where I saw some carp a while ago. My float lands quite safely and the wind melts away leaving a pleasant breeze.

Without warning, a wide mouth and head rises from the water just beyond my float. I can't see my bait so I watch patiently and observe the situation. My float slides away and I strike, standing up as I feel the vibrations of a fighting fish on the other end. My clutch clicks as the line is slowly released. My rod is bent double, Richard Walker's touch once again has been there to help the proceedings along. The carp kites one way and then the other as I slowly try to gain line. The carp dives, taking line with

him, and then I feel nothing. The carp has dived to the remaining weed beds. I pull and keep a constant pressure, hoping the carp will pull free. But nothing happens. I then let the line go slack, hoping the carp will free himself. Line starts to pour out as the fish tries to escape, but this time I strike up again, the fish swims free and we restart our battle. The fish is tiring and I start to reel him in. With his head raised I draw him slowly over the net. It looks like a good fish, as I raise the net up around it. Cradling it and holding the net by its arms and my rod, I struggle to the top of the bank of my swim and unhook the fish. The first glimpse of a caught fish is always either heart-warming or very disappointing in my experience. But this fish is beautiful – its underneath is orange and yellow, high-lighting and reflecting through its mirrors the colours of the day. It is just under seventeen pounds.

A quick thrust of his tail and he is away back to his home in the weeds.

Today is the earliest time in the year that I've ever caught a carp from the surface. Perhaps it reflects the mild winter we're having. While other ponds and rivers up the country are frozen and snowbound and anglers patiently wait for days or weeks for a bite, it seems that here the warm, wet winters agree with the carp, keeping them active all year round. In fact, looking back through my angling records, it seems I catch more carp in the autumn and winter months than I do in the summer. I think that this is to do with other anglers. In hot, dry weather, people like to fish and the carp get pressurized and are cautious about all unnatural baits. In the winter, anglers tend to stay at home in the warmth of their own homes, so the fish drop their defences. Today has proved this. In summer carp are very hard to catch on the surface of the Pond but today and the last week or so carp have been feeding freely from the surface.

Dick Walker was right to believe in 'thinking' the carp out. Making up theories and then putting them to the test. I do it all the time and so do many other anglers I know who aren't afraid of being thought different. Eventually we all reap the reward.

Today's fishing took me about an hour and a half to catch a very nice fish. It might sound a short time, but days, even weeks, have gone by without me actually fishing, just watching, learning, getting ready and working things out. Fishing needn't be like this, and to a lot it isn't, but days of thought and research are needed if you are to succeed and eventually catch the fish you are after. With fishing, as with most other things in life, you only get back what you are prepared to put in.

My LAST HOOK

17 |

For the last month or so I haven't touched this book. I've read interviews with authors before, and they have all said that the last chapter is always the hardest to write. I've worried about how to finish, as I think the end should be like a firework display, leaving the observer immensely happy, a grand finale of fish and thoughts.

My last chapter was about the end of winter and now it is well into spring, leaves are lush and freshly appearing where bare twigs once hung. Bluebells and buttercups adorn the hedgerows and are scattered all around the Pond. Daisies pop up from nowhere, looking up from grassy beds, and there, in the middle of all this beauty, is the Pond. Weed sits in the subsurface rousing the match-men's fury. They came and raked some of the weed out, and alas a lot of reed – I don't know why they did this as it would only encourage new growth – a week or so ago. The water level is down and it all seems to be perfect. For the last day or so the carp have spawned. Last year they were in the shallows spawning, but this year they're in the weed, right in the middle of the pond. Although the carp here are such prolific spawners there is never any small carp or fry. (There is a scientific reason for this, but I don't know exactly what it is.)

Today there are no fishermen. The sun is bright and beautiful so I'm off in my Indian canoe to explore the depths of reed, weed and water, along with my rod, reel, landing net and camera, to try and get some close-ups of basking and spawning carp.

I travel out towards where I've seen the carp spawn and, sure enough, six or seven sit wallowing in the sunshine. Their backs sit up right out of the water, making them look like a line of man-eaters waiting for their prey. A few yards past the carp, there is a dead common, which looks about fourteen pounds, that I net and bring into the canoe. It has been dead for a couple of days and the heat of the sun has putrefied it, making it smell a vile, stomach-churning stench. I cover it with my keepsack. I make plaster casts of any fish I find dead and then paint them as a record. I find plaster to be somewhat awkward to use and hard to paint and finish, so I'm experimenting at the moment with rubber latex to make the mould and resin to make the cast.

I now drift down towards where the reeds have been cut. I can see one or two smaller carp sunning themselves and then a sight which I've only seen about three times before – the biggest carp in the Pond! Every time I have caught a glimpse of him, he has been by the reeds. This carp is the biggest I've ever seen here. He's a mirror and his size dwarfs the other carp, making them look like roach and him a big bream standing out prominently and majestically. This is my chance to write the final chapter; this is the fish for which I've waited all my life on the Pond.

My hand quivers as I pinch a piece of bread flake onto my hook and cast – a perfect cast for once and the bread slowly sinks. Without hesitation, the mighty carp takes the bait, setting the trap as I pull up hard setting the hook. The carp bolts, causing my rod to bend in a severe arc. The clutch clicks as line comes from my reel. This is it!

The carp heads into the reeds, throwing the reeds into its path. My line goes slack and the hookless end floats in the air. I swear out loud again and again. My head aches, my stomach aches, my throat is dry. The carp of my dreams has gone. I sit and look at the end of the line. The hook's knot hadn't come undone and I hadn't felt the line cut or grate causing the line to snap, the fish must have been more powerful than I had imagined. I can't believe what has happened. In a billionth of a second, total happiness has turned into total defeat. My angling life was back to square one instead of the joy of catching the biggest carp in the Pond. That feeling of utter nothing-ness which comes after losing a big fish never fails to amaze me. When you are playing a big fish everything is exciting and nerve-racking, all the bodily functions working together, physical and mental processes grind-ing as adrenalin sets the high with dreams of a banked Leviathan coming to mind, then a snap, a hook pull and . . . nothing! The adrenalin drains away, my head thumps with disappointment and my heart sinks into my stom-ach, my whole body is trembling and shaking with the loss.

I slowly punt towards the bank. I've had enough of fishing. When I reach the bank I leave my tackle in the boat and wander home with the dead carp to put in the freezer ready for mounting. On the walk home I continue to swear at the world around me.

After putting the dead carp in the freezer, my hunger for angling returns and I go to my creel to get a new hook to replace the one I've lost. There is one hook left. I use a special sort of carp hook and I find that no other brand will do. Unfortunately, I can only get these hooks from Plymouth which is the nearest large city. I don't go there very often – it seems a waste of time and money to go there just for some hooks – so I look after the hooks I do have. Now I'm down to my last one!

When I get back to my boat I tie the new hook and set out again. I watch the area where the carp I'd lost had gone and hope I'll find him again. I decide to call him Dando after the ghost monk who haunts the estate, just as this fish has haunted me for so many years. As I mentioned earlier, I think the other anglers call this fish Big Red but I haven't seen a photo or seen that carp out of the water, and anyway, I prefer the name Dando!

I pull my canoe through the stumps of reeds and stare longingly into the shallow water, studying it for signs of life, and there, almost exactly where I'd lost him, sits Dando, half in and half out of a clump of reeds, trying to hide from the dangers above. I know it is Dando, firstly from his immense size and, secondly, from the scratch on the top of his head which I had noticed earlier, probably caused by spawning. This is surely my chance! As I've said, before today I've only seen him three times and now I'm having my second chance at catching him. I move the canoe very slowly until I am directly over him and then bait my hook and slowly lower it right in front of his mouth. He sucks it in and out, in and out, as if he is human and breathing through his mouth. In and out, again and again and again. Every time he sucks it in the bait goes a little further back into his mouth. He is obviously testing and feeling for the line and hook. The bait goes in . . . then out . . . then in. I am leaning on my arm and getting pins and needles, but I keep very still. The bait goes in and I strike, the hook is set again and Dando takes off. This time there is no sudden slackness. Dando thrashes about in the reeds, taking line which I retrieve.

I am starting to win the fight, I bring him closer and stretch and try to land him, but my boat moves. I try again, but every time I lean on the side to net the fish the canoe moves in the opposite direction. I hold the fish's head up and clamp the rod underneath my chin. I grip the reeds to pull me closer with one hand and I raise the landing net with the other, engulfing the fish. I've done it! I sigh and pull the landing net towards me and lift it into my boat and on to an unhooking mat and weigh sling. I cover the fish with another sling to keep it from injuring itself by flapping about on the boat. I don't look at the fish. I just punt in as quickly as I can. I lift the fish out of the boat and go to a soft grassy area to unwrap Dando. I am amazed at the size of his scales. I carefully make my way to his mouth and unhook it, and see my first hook. I retrieve it and thank my lucky stars that I have been saved from another trip into Plymouth for another week or two.

I weigh Dando. When I'd seen him swimming in the water, I'd estimated that he was about twenty-four pounds. The scales read twenty-three pounds and ten ounces. Many carp anglers reading this will turn their noses up or laugh at my joy at catching this fish. Indeed, I've caught bigger carp from other ponds and lost, as all anglers have, fish twice the size of Dando. But this is the fish that has been my personal target for years. I've dreamed about this day ever since I was a boy. If I caught the biggest fish from Wrasbury or Redmire, my face would be synonymous amongst anglers.

But now a feeling of loss overcomes me. What's left for the Pond and me now? Our relationship is perhaps not one of mystery any more. Perhaps the spirit has accepted me as part of it, like the kingfishers, water rats and carp themselves. Maybe I should leave the Pond to itself now and go and find another water to fall in love with. Perhaps give up carping on the Pond and fish for eels or the big rudd in the Blown-up? But that is tomorrow, this is today and there on the bank in front of me, lies the King of the Pond.